Printed in the United States
by Baker & Taylor Publisher Services

T0214303

Lecture Notes in Computer Science 11796

Founding Editors

Gerhard Goos
Karlsruhe Institute of Technology, Karlsruhe, Germany
Juris Hartmanis
Cornell University, Ithaca, NY, USA

Editorial Board Members

Elisa Bertino
Purdue University, West Lafayette, IN, USA
Wen Gao
Peking University, Beijing, China
Bernhard Steffen
TU Dortmund University, Dortmund, Germany
Gerhard Woeginger
RWTH Aachen, Aachen, Germany
Moti Yung
Columbia University, New York, NY, USA

More information about this series at http://www.springer.com/series/7412

Luping Zhou · Duygu Sarikaya ·
Seyed Mostafa Kia · Stefanie Speidel ·
Anand Malpani · Daniel Hashimoto ·
Mohamad Habes · Tommy Löfstedt ·
Kerstin Ritter · Hongzhi Wang (Eds.)

OR 2.0 Context-Aware Operating Theaters and Machine Learning in Clinical Neuroimaging

Second International Workshop, OR 2.0 2019
and Second International Workshop, MLCN 2019
Held in Conjunction with MICCAI 2019
Shenzhen, China, October 13 and 17, 2019
Proceedings

 Springer

Editors
Luping Zhou
University of Sydney
Sydney, NSW, Australia

Seyed Mostafa Kia ⓘ
Radboud University Medical Center
Nijmegen, The Netherlands

Anand Malpani ⓘ
Malone Center for Engineering in Healthcare
Johns Hopkins University
Baltimore, MD, USA

Mohamad Habes
University of Pennsylvania
Philadelphia, PA, USA

Kerstin Ritter
Charité-Universitätsmedizin Berlin
Berlin, Germany

Duygu Sarikaya ⓘ
University of Rennes 1
Rennes, France

Stefanie Speidel ⓘ
National Center for Tumor
Diseases (NCT/UCC)
Dresden, Germany

Daniel Hashimoto ⓘ
Harvard Medical School
Massachusetts General Hospital
Boston, MA, USA

Tommy Löfstedt
Umeå University
Umeå, Sweden

Hongzhi Wang
IBM Research - Almaden
San Jose, CA, USA

ISSN 0302-9743   ISSN 1611-3349 (electronic)
Lecture Notes in Computer Science
ISBN 978-3-030-32694-4   ISBN 978-3-030-32695-1 (eBook)
https://doi.org/10.1007/978-3-030-32695-1

LNCS Sublibrary: SL6 – Image Processing, Computer Vision, Pattern Recognition, and Graphics

© Springer Nature Switzerland AG 2019, corrected publication 2024
Chapter "Live Monitoring of Haemodynamic Changes with Multispectral Image Analysis" is licensed under the terms of the Creative Commons Attribution 4.0 International License (http://creativecommons.org/licenses/by/4.0/). For further details see license information in the chapter.
This work is subject to copyright. All rights are reserved by the Publisher, whether the whole or part of the material is concerned, specifically the rights of translation, reprinting, reuse of illustrations, recitation, broadcasting, reproduction on microfilms or in any other physical way, and transmission or information storage and retrieval, electronic adaptation, computer software, or by similar or dissimilar methodology now known or hereafter developed.
The use of general descriptive names, registered names, trademarks, service marks, etc. in this publication does not imply, even in the absence of a specific statement, that such names are exempt from the relevant protective laws and regulations and therefore free for general use.
The publisher, the authors and the editors are safe to assume that the advice and information in this book are believed to be true and accurate at the date of publication. Neither the publisher nor the authors or the editors give a warranty, expressed or implied, with respect to the material contained herein or for any errors or omissions that may have been made. The publisher remains neutral with regard to jurisdictional claims in published maps and institutional affiliations.

This Springer imprint is published by the registered company Springer Nature Switzerland AG
The registered company address is: Gewerbestrasse 11, 6330 Cham, Switzerland

Additional Workshop Editors

Satellite Events Chair

Kenji Suzuki
Tokyo Institute of Technology
Yokohama, Japan

Workshop Chairs

Hongen Liao
Tsinghua University
Beijing, China

Hayit Greenspan
Tel Aviv University
Tel Aviv, Israel

Challenge Chairs

Qian Wang
Shanghai Jiaotong University
Shanghai, China

Bram van Ginneken
Radboud University
Nijmegen, Netherlands

Tutorial Chair

Luping Zhou
University of Sydney
Sydney, Australia

International Workshop on OR 2.0 Context-Aware Operating Theaters, OR 2.0 2019

Duygu Sarikaya
University of Rennes I
Rennes, France

Anand Malpani
Johns Hopkins University
Baltimore, MD
USA

Stefanie Speidel
National Center for Tumor Diseases
Dresden, Germany

Daniel Hashimoto
Harvard Medical School
Boston, MA
USA

International Workshop on Machine Learning in Clinical Neuroimaging, MLCN 2019

Seyed Mostafa Kia
Radboud University Medical Center
Nijmegen, The Netherlands

Kerstin Ritter
Charité-Universitätsmedizin Berlin
Berlin
Germany

Hongzhi Wang
IBM Almaden Research Center
San Jose, CA
USA

Mohamad Habes
University of Pennsylvania
Philadelphia, MA
USA

Tommy Löfstedt
Umeå University
Umeå
Sweden

OR 2.0 2019 Preface

Surgical robotic tools and digitally enhanced operating theaters have been giving surgeons a helping hand for years. While they provide great control, precision, and flexibility to the surgeons, they do not yet address the cognitive assistance needs in the operating theater. We are on the verge of a new wave of innovations of artificial-intelligence-powered, context-aware operating theaters. We envision future operating theaters that are holistic and seamlessly integrated in the surgery process. They will monitor their environment by gathering multi-modal data from sources such as cameras, sensors, monitoring devices, patient profile and history, and they will respond accordingly. Although this could be realized by following pre-established rules, a better and more holistic way would be to develop context-aware systems that are able to perceive and reason, make sense of ongoing processes, project outcomes of a number of possible actions that could be taken within this context, provide quantitative support to aid the decision making process, evaluate the outcomes of the action taken, and use this information for the next steps. Advances in context-awareness can answer these needs and complement the surgical team by assisting the surgical procedures, providing real-time guidance during complex tasks and unexpected events.

This workshop aims to highlight the potential use of, with a particular focus but not limited to, machine vision and perception, robotics, surgical simulation and modeling, multi-modal data fusion and visualization, image analysis, advanced imaging, advanced display technologies, human-computer interfaces, sensors, wearable and implantable electronics and robots, visual attention models, cognitive models, decision support networks to enhance surgical procedural assistance, context-awareness and team communication in the operating theater, human-robot collaborative systems, and surgical training and assessment.

OR 2.0 2019 was the Second International Workshop on Context-Aware Surgical Theaters, organized as a satellite event of the Medical Image Computing and Computer Assisted Intervention (MICCAI 2019) conference in Shenzhen, China. The first International OR 2.0 Context-Aware Operating Theaters Workshop was held in September 2018, in Granada, Spain in conjunction with MICCAI 2018. As we received quite positive feedback from our participants, especially from early career researchers both from academia and industry, and we also received submissions from research labs all over the world, we decided to organize a second workshop. Our workshop is highly correlated with MICCAI 2019's focus on implementation of, and training for, computer-assisted intervention approaches. This year, we expanded our board with an Industrial Board from various companies that work on related topics. We also introduced bench to OR awards along with our best paper awards, which are given to works that bring novel concepts to operating theaters that will increase context-awareness, and have potential to be easily translated into clinical applications. With our workshop, we aim to define the future technologies of the operating theater.

We wish to thank all the OR 2.0 2019 authors for their participation and our board for their feedback and commitment to the workshop. We are very grateful to our sponsor Intuitive Surgery for their support since the beginning of our workshop series.

The proceedings of the workshop are published as a joint LNCS volume of satellite events organized in conjunction with MICCAI 2019. The OR 2.0 2019 proceedings contain six high-quality papers that were selected through a double-blind peer-review process. All submissions were peer reviewed by at least three reviewers who are experts on related topics. Awards were based on the nominations made by the reviewers, and the votes of the Industrial Board. In addition to the papers presented in this LNCS volume, the workshop featured three keynote talks from Dr. Qi Dou (Imperial College London, UK), Dr. Murilo M. Marinho (University of Tokyo, Japan), and Dr. Guangzhi Wang (Tsinghua University, China), who also served as the vice president of the Chinese Society of Biomedical Engineering and the Chinese Association of Medical Imaging Technology.

This volume features accepted papers on topics of a laparoscopic scene segmentation model with modified Xception as encoder, and a decoder for feature aggregation, an automatic trajectory planning method for endovascular procedures using shape regularized U-Net and statistical optimization, a surgical image desmoking method that does not require the use of synthetic data generation, and utilizes cycle-GAN and atrous convolutions, an unsupervised temporal video segmentation method as an auxiliary task to improve the performance of remaining surgery duration prediction, an end-to-end deep learning pipeline for multi-spectral image analysis to obtain intra-operative functional information in real-time, and cyber-physical system concepts for the intelligent operating theater. More details on our workshop program are available on our website: https://or20.univ-rennes1.fr/.

October 2019

Duygu Sarikaya
Stefanie Speidel
Anand Malpani
Daniel Hashimoto

OR 2.0 2019 Organization

Organizing Board

Duygu Sarikaya	University of Rennes I, France
Stefanie Speidel	National Center for Tumor Diseases, Germany
Anand Malpani	Johns Hopkins University, USA
Daniel Hashimoto	Harvard Medical School, USA

Industrial Board

Imanol Luengo	Touch Surgery, UK
Omid Mohareri	Intuitive Surgery, USA
Lars Mündermann	KARL STORZ SE & Co. KG, Germany
Cyrill von Tiesenhausen	Kuka Roboter GmbH, Germany

Advisory Board

Chee Kong Chui	National University of Singapore, Singapore
Paolo Fiorini	University of Verona, Italy
Pheng-Ann Heng	The Chinese University of Hong Kong, SAR China
Pierre Jannin	University of Rennes I, France
Ken Masamune	Tokyo Women's Medical University, Japan
Thomas Neumuth	Innovation Center Computer Assisted Surgery, Germany
Nicolas Padoy	University of Strasbourg, France
Sandrine de Ribaupierre	University of Western Ontario, Canada
Marco Zenati	Harvard Medical School, USA
Guoyan Zheng	Shanghai Jiao Tong University, China

MLCN 2019 Preface

Recent advances in neuroimaging and machine learning provide an exceptional opportunity for researchers to discover complex relationships between the brain, behaviors, and mental disorders. Neuroimaging techniques such as structural and functional magnetic resonance imaging (s/fMRI) can measure non-invasively the morphology as well as the resting state or task-induced neural correlates from different brain regions in a limited period. While classical univariate statistics are unable to exploit complex multivariate patterns in neuroimaging data, advanced machine learning approaches can be employed to benefit from this wealth of information to provide a deeper understanding of the underlying neurobiological mechanisms and improve clinical decision making. Although machine learning techniques were first successfully applied to clinical neuroimaging data a decade ago, to date, there has been limited translation to the clinic. Reasons for this include the lack of available labeled clinical data, a reduction in quality for clinical imaging set-ups, and a lack of harmonization for related clinical data sets acquired from different sites.

The Second International Workshop on Machine Learning in Clinical Neuroimaging (MLCN 2019) was held in conjunction with MICCAI 2019, with a special focus on addressing the problems of applying machine learning to large and multi-site clinical neuroimaging datasets. The workshop aimed to bring together experts in both machine learning and clinical neuroimaging to discuss and hopefully bridge the existing challenges of applied machine learning in clinical neuroscience.

The call for papers for the MLCN 2019 workshop was released on April 14, 2019, with the manuscript submission deadline set to July 14, 2019. The received manuscripts went through a double-blind review process by MLCN 2019 Program Committee members. Each paper was thoroughly reviewed by at least four reviewers and the top six papers were qualified for publication. The accepted contributions addressed the application of machine learning to generally small sample size neuroimaging data through novel methodologies for data harmonization and transfer learning.

In the end, we would like to thank the MLCN 2019 Steering Committee for their enlightening guidance in organizing this event. We wish to also thank all authors for their valuable contributions and the MLCN 2019 Program Committee for their precious effort in evaluating the submissions.

October 2019

Mohamad Habes
Seyed Mostafa Kia
Tommy Löfstedt
Kerstin Ritter
Hongzhi Wang

MLCN 2019 Organization

Steering Committee

Christos Davatzikos   University of Pennsylvania, USA
Edouard Duchesnay   CEA NeuroSpin, France
Andre Marquand   Radboud University Medical Center, The Netherlands
Emma Robinson   King's College London, UK

Organizing Committee

Mohamad Habes   University of Pennsylvania, USA
Seyed Mostafa Kia   Radboud University Medical Center, The Netherlands
Tommy Löfstedt   Umeå University, Sweden
Kerstin Ritter   Charité-Universitätsmedizin Berlin, Germany
Hongzhi Wang   IBM Almaden Research Center, USA

Program Committee

Ehsan Adeli   Stanford University, USA
Andre Altmann   University College London, UK
Richard Dinga   Radboud University Medical Center, The Netherlands
Walter Hugo Lopez Pinaya   King's College London, UK
Hangfan Liu   University of Pennsylvania, USA
Marco Lorenzi   Université Côte d'Azur, France
Emanuele Olivetti   Bruno Kessler Foundation, Italy
Han Peng   University of Oxford, UK
Pradeep Reddy Raamana   University of Toronto, Canada
Jane Maryam Rondina   University College London, UK
Haochang Shou   University of Pennsylvania, USA
Aristeidis Sotiras   Washington University, USA
Erdem Varol   Columbia University, USA
Thomas Wolfers   Radboud University Medical Center, The Netherlands

Contents

Proceedings of the 2nd International Workshop on OR 2.0 Context-Aware Operating Theaters (OR 2.0 2019)

Feature Aggregation Decoder
for Segmenting Laparoscopic Scenes

Abdolrahim Kadkhodamohammadi[1]([✉]), Imanol Luengo[1], Santiago Barbarisi[1],
Hinde Taleb[1], Evangello Flouty[1], and Danail Stoyanov[1,2]

[1] Digital Surgery Ltd., 230 City Road, London EC1V 2QY, UK
rahim.mohammadi@touchsurgery.com
[2] Wellcome/EPSRC Centre for Interventional and Surgical Sciences,
University College London, London, UK

Abstract. Laparoscopic scene segmentation is one of the key building
blocks required for developing advanced computer assisted interventions
and robotic automation. Scene segmentation approaches often rely on
encoder-decoder architectures that encode a representation of the input
to be decoded to semantic pixel labels. In this paper, we propose to
use the deep *Xception* model for the encoder and a simple yet effective decoder that relies on a feature aggregation module. Our feature
aggregation module constructs a mapping function that reuses and transfers encoder features and combines information across all feature scales
to build a richer representation that keeps both high-level context and
low-level boundary information. We argue that this aggregation module
enables us to simplify the decoder and reduce the number of parameters
in the decoder. We have evaluated our approach on two datasets and our
experimental results show that our model outperforms state-of-the-art
models on the same experimental setup and significantly improves the
previous results, 98.44% vs 89.00%, on the EndoVis'15 dataset.

Keywords: Semantic segmentation · Minimally invasive surgery ·
Surgical vision

1 Introduction

Laparoscopic techniques have become a paradigm in modern interventions due
to the numerous benefits over laparotomy such as shorter hospital stay, less
scars, reduced postsurgical pain and faster recovery. Visualising the anatomy in
high definition with bright illumination through the laparoscope also provides a
magnified, detailed view of the surgical site that can be seen in 3D. However,
minimally invasive surgery comes at the cost of restricting surgeon's range of
motion and imposing altered hand-eye coordination [16]. As a result, significant
efforts in computer assisted interventions (CAI) have been directed at tools to
enhance surgeons' capabilities through robotics, image guidance and surgical

© Springer Nature Switzerland AG 2019
L. Zhou et al. (Eds.): OR 2.0 2019/MLCN 2019, LNCS 11796, pp. 3–11, 2019.
https://doi.org/10.1007/978-3-030-32695-1_1

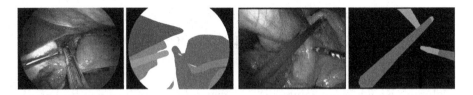

Fig. 1. Sample color and label images from LapSleeve and EndoVis'15 datasets, respectively. (Color figure online)

data science [5,10,13,14]. Laparoscopic scene segmentation is an essential building block in vision based CAI and is required to enable applications needing full surgical scene understanding [2,6].

Scene segmentation is a fundamental vision problem that is now tackled using deep Convolutional Neural Networks (CNNs). Features driving segmentation learned using deep CNN outperform handcrafted features like SIFT and HOG [8]. Fully Convolutional Networks (FCNs) can construct segmentation models that are learned in an end-to-end manner [12] using AlexNet [11] as the feature encoder and relying on transposed convolutions as the decoder to predict pixel-level labels. The FCN model can be extended by improving either the encoder or the decoder to achieve better performance [3,7]. *U-Net* is one of the popular architectures adopting FCN for segmenting biomedical images [15]. The U-net encoder consists of a sequence of convolutional blocks that map and downsample the input by a factor of two and the decoder applies a sequence of similar blocks, but upsamples the output at the end of each block. *ToolNet* [7] follows a similar architecture, but simplifies the decoder to reduce the computation burden. The decoder concatenates the output of each encoder blocks and computes a segmentation loss on the output of each block to provide stage-wise supervision. While powerful, these architectures are relatively shallow and have a limited feature receptive field, which limits performance in complex surgical scenes.

In this paper, we introduce a novel decoder architecture that reuses the rich representations extracted by the *Xception* model [4]. This builds deep, rich representations while it reduces the number of parameters by using depthwise separable convolutions as shown by DeepLabv3+ [3], the top performer on Pascal segmentation challenge at the moment [1]. Our decoder relies on a feature aggregation module to incorporate information across all feature channels and construct a mapping function that selects and combines the most informative channels. This aggregation module allows reuse of the multi-scale features extracted at different Xception modules and construction of a representation that preserves semantic information along with detailed object boundaries. Previous works [3,7,12] have also explored the idea of reusing multi-scale features computed by the encoder but only with a decoder that reuses features in-between a series of convolutions and upsampling blocks. This introduces more parameters to the decoder and hence requires more training data. Instead, our feature aggregation decoder constructs a channel-wise mixing function and removes the

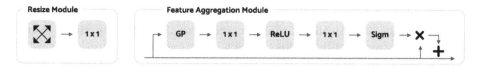

Fig. 2. The core modules of our decoder: left, a block to resize the output of Xception modules to the same size; right, feature aggregation module to learn a mapping function for transferring and combining feature channels.

need for multi-layer convolutions. We evaluate our approach on two datasets: *EndoVis'15* and Laparoscopic Sleeve gastrectomy, hereafter called *LapSleeve*. Figure 1 shows sample images. Our experimental results show that the proposed decoder outperforms the more complex segmentation network of [3] on the same experimental setup. Our model also significantly advances the state of the art results on EndoVis'15 dataset.

2   Method

Most recent scene segmentation approaches are based on FCN [3,12]. These approaches are following the encoder-decoder design where sequences of convolutional blocks are used as both encoder and decoder. We argue that deep CNN encoders can encode both low-level and high-level information and a decoder can reuse this information without the need for deep multi-stage decoders. We therefore propose to use a deep CNN encoder and propose a simple feature aggregation encoder to perform scene segmentation, which are explained next.

2.1   Xception Encoder

The Xception network has been originally proposed for image classification and has achieved promising results on ImageNet [4]. This network benefits from depthwise separable convolutions to reduce the number parameters. Chollet in [4] shows that separable convolutions also allow using the model parameters more efficiently. The Xception architecture consists of entry, middle and exit flows, which are built by using sequences of Xception modules with different numbers of output channels, stride sizes and residual connection types. In this paper, we use the modified aligned Xception model of [3], which was adapted for image segmentation. The modifications are: (1) doubling the number modules in the middle flow; (2) replacing max pooling operations with separable convolution with stride; (3) adding batch normalisation and ReLU activation after each 3×3 convolution; (4) extracting multi-resolution feature maps using *atrous convolution*. From the modified Xception module, we do not use atrous convolution. We instead build a multi-scale feature map by reusing the features computed by Xception modules at different scales. More specifically, we reuse the output of all Xception modules in the entry flow and the last module in the middle as well as exit flows. The entry flow modules have narrow receptive fields and are therefore more likely to capture low-level features such as texture and boundary information [15]. Meanwhile modules close to the output of the network benefit from larger receptive fields, hence wider context, that can theoretically enable constructing high-level representations for discriminating semantic categories [3]. We use our feature aggregation module to predict image pixel labels by assembling this low and high-level information.

2.2 Feature Aggregation Decoder

Our decoder utilises two modules to map representations into image pixel labels, shown in Fig. 2. We use the resize module at the output of the selected Xception modules for first resizing all the feature channels to be 1/16 of the input size and for fixing the number of output channels to 256. Bilinear interpolation is used to scale feature channels. The second module is the feature aggregation module. This module is designed to first capture global information and second construct a mapping function across all scales.

We aggregate information per channel by using global average pooling as a way of summarising global image information captured by each feature channel. We use these concise channel representations to learn a function for mapping information across channels. A similar idea has also been explored in [9] to model interdependency between channels inside a module. However, we argue that this operation can be used to learn dependency among features coming from different modules and recalibrate them to build a better representation. In our case, the benefit is not only aggregating information across scales, but also reducing the number of parameters and the computation burden at the decoder by effectively reusing extracted features. More formally, we can define the output of global average pooling as X and write the aggregation function as:

$$f(X) = \sigma(\rho(X * W_1 + \beta_1) * W_2 + \beta_2), \tag{1}$$

where σ is the standard logistic sigmoid function, ρ is the ReLU function, W_i and β_i are representing weight and bias vectors, respectively. This allows us to learn a nonlinear function, which incorporates channel-wise dependencies and relationships. This function can therefore put more emphases on some channels and learn a mapping function to calibrate feature channels. As function parameters are learned by optimising a segmentation loss, it learns to assemble the multi-scale features extracted at different parts of the encoder, which enables combining context and boundaries information. Finally, we apply a 1×1 convolution layer to the output of the feature aggregation module to refine and reduce the number of feature channels to 256. Our experiments show that this extra layer makes the training easier.

Table 1. EndoVis'15 results. The evaluation results are presented as per the splits provided with the dataset.

Metric	[2] DSC	DeepLabv3+ [3]			Feature Aggregation Decoder		
	DSC	DSC	mean DSC	mean IOU	DSC	mean DSC	mean IOU
OP1	-	98.41	95.15	91.02	98.83	95.85	92.22
OP2	-	98.36	94.89	90.58	98.01	95.03	90.78
OP3	-	98.42	95.22	91.15	98.76	96.08	92.63
OP4	-	98.18	94.41	90.01	98.31	95.2	91.09
OP5-OP6	-	98.0	94.66	90.17	98.3	94.73	90.32
Average	89.00	98.27	94.87	90.59	98.44	95.38	91.41

3   Experimental Results and Discussions

We implemented our approach using TensorFlow and perform all experiments on a Linux machine equipped with two NVIDIA GTX 1080 Ti GPUs. We optimise our networks using stochastic gradient decent. We use *poly* policy as learning rate scheduler [3] with the start learning rate of 0.0005 and finetune batch normalisation parameters. For the Xception backbone, we initialise the weight from a model trained on PASCAL VOC 2012 segmentation benchmark. Our resize module always scales the images to be 1/16 of the original image size.

For evaluation of our approach, we rely on two datasets: EndoVis'15 segmentation challenge and a laparoscopic sleeve gastrectomy dataset (LapSleeve). We use the EndoVis'15 rigid instrument dataset [2]. This dataset is generated from six laparoscopic colorectal surgeries. From each surgery, 50 frames are annotated. The train set includes the first 40 frames from OP1 to OP4 and the rest of the frames constructs the test set. A sample frame is shown in Fig. 1.

The LapSleeve dataset is generated from recordings of five laparoscopic sleeve gastrectomy procedures. We have randomly selected 600 to 900 frames from each video during the stomach dissection phase. In total, we have chosen 3600 frames. All these frames are annotated to provide full pixel-level segmentation masks. The dataset contains 14 class labels, namely stapler tip, stapler handle, stapler trigger, atraumatic grasper handle, atraumatic grasper tip, liver retractor, ligasure tip, ligasure handle, marylands tip, marylands handle, bandage, liver, stomach and background. We used all 750 frames from one of the videos as the test set and the rest as the training set.

We assessed the performance of our model by computing pixel intersection over union averaged across all classes (mean IOU). In case of EndoVis'15, we also compute the Dice Similarity Coefficient (DSC) as in [2], which is computed among prediction and ground-truth. As this is biased towards classes with high number of instances, we report average DSC across all classes (mean DSC).

Table 2. LapSleeve results. The mean IOU metric is used to compare the performance of our Feature Aggregation Decoder (FAD) with DeepLabv3+ on the same experimental. Different variants of our FAD are also evaluated. See the text for explanation.

	DeepLabv3+	FAD	FAD[-1CNN]	FAD[+1CNN]	FAD[-Add]	FAD[1/8]
mean IOU	42.76	47.81	45.74	46.88	46.16	41.54

EndoVis'15. We evaluate our model on the EndoVis'15 dataset following the experimental setup suggested in [2]. In other words, we follow a leave-one-surgery-out fashion, where frames from the test surgery are not used during training. We thus train five different models to evaluate on the different subsets provided in the test set. Table 1 presents the evaluation results in comparison to results of two other methods. Bodenstedt et al. [2] summarised the performance of the approaches participated in the EndoVis'15 challenge on instrument segmentation and tracking challenge. They obtained the best results by merging prediction results from several approaches using the STAPLE algorithm. In [2], the DSC metric is used to evaluate the performance of models in discriminating tools vs background[1]. As the DSC is however sensitive to the number of instances per class and the dataset is extremely unbalanced, where $\sim$ 70%–90% is the background class, we report mean DSC and also mean IOU that tends to penalise more wrong detections. In addition, we have reported the results of finetuned DeepLabv3+ initialised from a model trained on PASCAL VOC 2012. Our feature aggregation decoder preforms similarly to the DeepLabv3+, but always better, on the same experimental setup. This indicates that our decoder is capable of effectively aggregating information across different scales. Furthermore, our model achieves the DSC of 98.44%, which significantly outperforms the best model in [2].

Laparoscopic Sleeve. We use LapSleeve to train and evaluate our feature aggregation decoder and DeepLabv3+. All weights are initialised from models trained on PASCAL VOC 2012. The evaluation results on the LapSleeve dataset are presented in Table 2. Because of the higher complexity of LapSleeve that includes more classes and body organ segmentation classes, the performance of both models has dropped on this dataset compared to EndoVis'15 results. However, our model improves the performance by 5% over DeepLabv3+ on the same experimental setup. While DeepLabv3+ performs slightly better in segmenting body organs (80.01 vs 79.83), we found that our model is better in discriminating tool tips and tool handles. We should note that a handle and a tip of tool are in the same semantic group and only low-level edge information can help to distinguish these classes. Even though, given *enough* training data one can expect to retrieve this information from the presentation built at the end of encoder,

---

[1] Even though this dataset has been annotated for shaft, manipulator and background classes, the author of [2] confirms that shaft and manipulator are merged. We also merge these classes during our experiments.

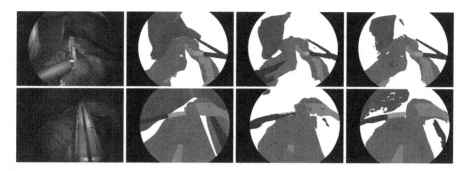

Fig. 3. Qualitative results: input image, label, DeepLabv3+ and our model. The predicted pixel-wise semantic labels are color coded. (Color figure online)

this information is often better captured at shallower layers of the encoder. Our higher precision in discriminating tool tips from handles underlines the benefits of our aggregation decoder in reusing multi-scale features across the encoder as opposed to DeepLabv3+, which tries to obtain all this information at the end of the encoder.

Figure 3 shows two sample frames along with corresponding labels and predictions. Our model is better in distinguishing grasper shaft from tip. The sample frame in the first row shows an example, where our model has successfully used low-level information to detect the stapler trigger. We have also used this dataset to evaluate different parameters of our model presented in Table 2. The performance of our model degrades dramatically when the resize module scales feature channels to 1/8 of the original image (FAD[1/8]). We believe that it is due to noise introduced by upsampling deep feature representations at the middle and the exit flows of Xception. Excluding the residual connection (FAD[-ADD]) also decreases the performance, which agrees with the findings in [9]. We remove (FAD[-1CNN]) and add (FAD[+1CNN]) a convolution layer after the feature aggregation module. The performance drops in both cases. Removing the convolution layer degrades the performance more, indicating that this layer is needed for reducing the number of channels in the representation built by the aggregation module and for converging to a better model.

4   Conclusions

In this paper, we proposed a simple yet effective decoder to perform laparoscopic scene segmentation. We use the modified aligned Xception model as our encoder. Our decoder relies on an aggregation module to reuse and calibrate representations extracted by the encoder at different scales. This aggregation module allows us to select the most informative feature channels and reuse them effectively for predicting pixel-level semantic labels. Our experiments on two different datasets highlights the effectiveness of our decoder. Our model significantly advances the state-of-the-art results on EndoVis'15 and achieves 98.44% DSC. We believe that the forward nature of our decoder enables systematic study of features at different modules that would boost the explainablility of our model and it would be interesting to look at this aspect in future work.

References

1. Pascal VOC 2012: segmentation leaderboard. http://host.robots.ox.ac.uk/leaderboard/displaylb.php?challengeid=11&compid=6. Accessed March 2019
2. Bodenstedt, S., et al.: Comparative evaluation of instrument segmentation and tracking methods in minimally invasive surgery. arXiv preprint arXiv:1805.02475 (2018)
3. Chen, L.-C., Zhu, Y., Papandreou, G., Schroff, F., Adam, H.: Encoder-decoder with atrous separable convolution for semantic image segmentation. In: Ferrari, V., Hebert, M., Sminchisescu, C., Weiss, Y. (eds.) ECCV 2018. LNCS, vol. 11211, pp. 833–851. Springer, Cham (2018). https://doi.org/10.1007/978-3-030-01234-2_49
4. Chollet, F.: Xception: deep learning with depthwise separable convolutions. In: Conference on Computer Vision and Pattern Recognition (CVPR), pp. 1800–1807. IEEE, July 2017
5. da Costa Rocha, C., Padoy, N., Rosa, B.: Self-supervised surgical tool segmentation using kinematic information. In: International Conference on Robotics and Automation (ICRA). IEEE (2019)
6. D'Ettorre, C., et al.: Automated pick-up of suturing needles for robotic surgical assistance. In: International Conference on Robotics and Automation (ICRA), pp. 1370–1377. IEEE (2018)
7. García-Peraza-Herrera, L.C., et al.: ToolNet: holistically-nested real-time segmentation of robotic surgical tools. In: International Conference on Intelligent Robots and Systems (IROS), pp. 5717–5722. IEEE, September 2017
8. Girshick, R., Donahue, J., Darrell, T., Malik, J.: Rich feature hierarchies for accurate object detection and semantic segmentation. In: Conference on Computer Vision and Pattern Recognition (CVPR), pp. 580–587. IEEE (2014)
9. Hu, J., Shen, L., Sun, G.: Squeeze-and-excitation networks. In: Conference on Computer Vision and Pattern Recognition (CVPR). IEEE, June 2018
10. Jin, A., et al.: Tool detection and operative skill assessment in surgical videos using region-based convolutional neural networks. In: Winter Conference on Applications of Computer Vision (WACV), pp. 691–699, March 2018
11. Krizhevsky, A., Sutskever, I., Hinton, G.E.: Imagenet classification with deep convolutional neural networks. In: Advances in Neural Information Processing Systems, pp. 1097–1105 (2012)
12. Long, J., Shelhamer, E., Darrell, T.: Fully convolutional networks for semantic segmentation. In: Conference on Computer Vision and Pattern Recognition (CVPR), pp. 3431–3440. IEEE (2015)
13. Maier-Hein, L., et al.: Why rankings of biomedical image analysis competitions should be interpreted with care. Nat. Commun. 9(1), 5217 (2018)
14. Münzer, B., Schoeffmann, K., Böszörmenyi, L.: Content-based processing and analysis of endoscopic images and videos: a survey. Multimedia Tools Appl. 77(1), 1323–1362 (2018)

15. Ronneberger, O., Fischer, P., Brox, T.: U-Net: convolutional networks for biomedical image segmentation. In: Navab, N., Hornegger, J., Wells, W.M., Frangi, A.F. (eds.) MICCAI 2015. LNCS, vol. 9351, pp. 234–241. Springer, Cham (2015). https://doi.org/10.1007/978-3-319-24574-4_28

16. Wilson, M., Coleman, M., McGrath, J.: Developing basic hand-eye coordination skills for laparoscopic surgery using gaze training. BJU Int. **105**(10), 1356–1358 (2010)

Preoperative Planning for Guidewires Employing Shape-Regularized Segmentation and Optimized Trajectories

Johannes Fauser[1(✉)], Moritz Fuchs[1], Ahmed Ghazy[2], Bernhard Dorweiler[2], and Anirban Mukhopadhyay[1]

[1] Department of Computer Science, Technische Universität Darmstadt, Darmstadt, Germany
johannes.fauser@gris.tu-darmstadt.de
[2] University Medical Center, Johannes Gutenberg University Mainz, Mainz, Germany

Abstract. Upcoming robotic interventions for endovascular procedures can significantly reduce the high radiation exposure currently endured by surgeons. Robotically driven guidewires replace manual insertion and leave the surgeon the task of planning optimal trajectories based on segmentation of associated risk structures. However, such a pipeline brings new challenges. While Deep learning based segmentation such as U-Net can achieve outstanding Dice scores, it fails to provide suitable results for trajectory planning in annotation scarce environments. We propose a preoperative pipeline featuring a shape regularized U-Net that extracts coherent anatomies from pixelwise predictions. It uses Rapidly-exploring Random Trees together with convex optimization for locally optimal planning. Our experiments on two publicly available data sets evaluate the complete pipeline. We show the benefits of our approach in a functional evaluation including both segmentation and planning metrics: While we achieve comparable Dice, Hausdorff distances and planning metrics such as success rate of motion planning algorithms are significantly better than U-Net.

Keywords: Preoperative planning · Shape regularization · Functional evaluation · Endovascular procedures

1 Introduction

Minimally-invasive procedures for stenting or treatment of aneurysms use guidewires [1,2] to provide easier access through complex vascular structures. With these tools, and a combination of both fluoroscopy and CT-images as visual guidance, a surgeon navigates a catheter to difficult-to-reach anatomical sites such as side branches of the aorta or pulmonary arteries. However, regular use of CT or x-ray acquisition exposes clinicians over time to accumulated high doses

© Springer Nature Switzerland AG 2019
L. Zhou et al. (Eds.): OR 2.0 2019/MLCN 2019, LNCS 11796, pp. 12–20, 2019.
https://doi.org/10.1007/978-3-030-32695-1_2

of radiation. Upcoming robotically driven guidewires [3] have the potential to significantly reduce this exposure but require complex preoperative planning.

An efficient preoperative pipeline that transfers the burden of segmentation and trajectory planning to automated algorithms while keeping the surgeon in control of crucial parts is vital for the success of these new robotic approaches.

We consider two example anatomies for endovascular procedures, aorta and pulmonary arteries (Fig. 1), to evaluate a preoperative pipeline including segmentation of risk structures and nonlinear trajectory planning. To the best of our knowledge, no complete pipeline of preoperative planning for endovascular procedures has been proposed so far. Azizi et al. [4] exploited centerline extraction to search for collision-free piecewise linear trajectories serving as a guidance for tools. They evaluated their segmentation on five cases for arteries and a 3D model of a porcine portal artery. Chi et al. introduced reinforcement learning to further optimize paths on centerline extraction [3]. Their evaluation on three aortic arch phantoms considered navigation along trajectories only. Most recently, Fauser et al. [5] investigated sequential convex optimization for trajectory optimization in guidewire procedures. Their method was evaluated on the SegThor data set [6] but uses ground truth segmentation as a basis for computation.

In this paper, we investigate a full preoperative pipeline including both segmentation and trajectory planning. We identify three key challenges for complete evaluation:

1. Guaranteeing coherent shapes after segmentation, i.e. without fragmentation or isolated regions, because these interfere with collision detection.
2. Interactive definition of the motion planning problem. This includes placement of start and goal regions. But also correction of surface meshes, if neighboring labels (e.g. right ventricle and atrium) result in boundaries between structures where naturally there are transitions.
3. Providing a clinically optimal solution if motion planning algorithms do not guarantee optimality.

To address the first issue, we adapt the shape-regularized U-Net approach of [7,8]: In data-scarce environments with only few annotated training images, deep learning architectures like U-Net [9] fail to guarantee coherent boundaries due to pixelwise prediction. Active Shape Models (ASM) [10] on the other hand intrinsically provide strong topological assumptions in terms of shapes but need proper initialization. A combination of both, where U-Net initializes ASMs [8], provides the best of both worlds: high accuracy and anatomically realistic shapes. For the second issue, we rely on the 3D environment provided by the resulting surface models. Here, a surgeon can efficiently define start and goal regions for trajectory planning as well as cutting holes into the existing surface meshes using adequate interaction. We tackle the last issue by using Bi-directional Rapidly-exploring Random Trees [11] with Bézier-Splines as steering functions [12] to compute multiple feasible trajectories. An iteration of sequential convex optimization [5,13] improves clearance to obstacles for these paths. We then rely on the surgeon to identify the clinically optimal solution.

In our experiments we conduct a functional evaluation of the pipeline combining metrics on downstream tasks (trajectory planning) along with Dice and Hausdorff distances as segmentation metrics. Our results show that with shape regularized obstacles successful preoperative planning is possible.

■ Aorta ■ Heart ▣ Esophagus ■ Trachea ■ Pulmonary Artery ■ Left Ventricle
■ Right Ventricle ▥ Left Atrium ■ Right Atrium ▥ Myocardium

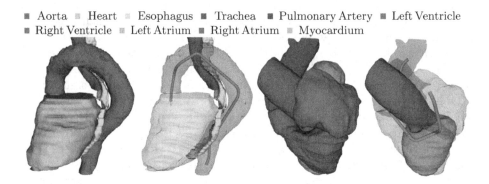

Fig. 1. A trajectory through left: the aorta to the heart for a SegThor sample and right: the right atrium and ventricle to the pulmonary arteries for a MMWHS sample.

2   Materials and Methods

Data: We evaluate our proposed framework on two publicly available data sets. First, using the 40 3D-CT thorax scans of this year's SegTHOR challenge [6] with corresponding label images identifying heart, aorta, esophagus and trachea. Secondly, using partial data of 2017's MMWHS challenge [14], specifically the two CT training sets offering a total of 20 3D-CT scans with corresponding label images discriminating between left ventricle, atrium and myocardium, right ventricle and atrium as well as ascending aorta and pulmonary artery (Fig. 1).

General Procedure: Both anatomies offer the possibility of evaluating the preoperative pipeline shown in Fig. 2: Based on a CT scan, a segmentation algorithm automatically extracts organs at risk while guaranteeing realistic shaped boundaries. In the resulting 3D anatomy the surgeon defines start and target states for the designated procedure. A motion planning algorithm then computes feasible trajectories for the instrument which are optimized regarding clearance to obstacles. This procedure automates laborious tasks, while at the same time giving the surgeon control over crucial parts of the pipeline.

Segmentation: Similar to [7], we rely on Deep Learning to properly initialize Active Shape Models (ASM).

U-Net: Taking a slice-by-slice approach, we first predict axial, sagittal and coronal slices using three individual 2D U-Nets $\mathcal{U}_A, \mathcal{U}_S, \mathcal{U}_C$, respectively, and apply majority voting on these three results to receive an initial 3D segmentation image $I^{\mathcal{U}}$. For trajectory planning, however, we need surface meshes of the detected structures' boundaries. Using the Marching Cubes algorithm on $I^{\mathcal{U}}$, surface meshes $M_i^{\mathcal{U}}, 0 \leq i \leq N$, for each of the N organs are extracted ($N = 4$ for SegThor, $N = 7$ for MMWHS). All three U-Nets consist of 5 levels, each implementing one separable 3×3 convolution layer followed by ReLU activation and doubling the number of feature channels starting with 16 channels. A reverted sequence of 5 levels combining up-convolutions and skip connections finishes with a soft-max activation for a final segmentation output. We use RMSProp as optimizer with a learning rate of 0.0001 and train for 30 epochs.

ASM: For each of the risk structures we create a statistical shape model (SSM) $\mathcal{S}_i, 0 \leq i \leq N$. For correspondence search, we extract ground truth meshes M_i^{GT} using first Marching Cubes on label images and then coarsening these shapes to 5000 landmarks [15]. For initialization of an individual active shape model (ASM), we nonrigidly register the mean shape of its SSM to U-Net's mesh result $M_i^{\mathcal{U}}$. In particular, we use a Probabilistic ASM (PASM) which iteratively adapts its shape using an energy function that weighs between the projection into shape space and image information [16]. This results in a final segmentation mask $I^{\mathcal{P}}$ and corresponding meshes $M_i^{\mathcal{P}}, 0 \leq i \leq N$.

Trajectory Planning: We rely on the surgeon to interactively define start and goal for the guidewire. We use Bi-directional Rapidly-exploring Trees (Bi-RRT) to find initial solutions and sequential convex optimization (SCO) for enhancement of clearance to risk structures.

Interactive Setup: Given the 3D environment of risk structures, a surgeon initializes the motion planning problem. For guidewire planning in endovascular procedures, we specifically consider

- a start state $q_S \in C = \mathbb{R}^3 \times SO(2)$ to enforce strict position and direction,
- a goal state $q_G \in C$ to enforce the same at the target,
- an upper curvature constraint $\kappa_{max} \geq 0$, representing the maximum bending capability of the guidewire,
- a safety distance d_{min}, combining the guidewires size and a safety margin to account for navigation and segmentation errors. We model the guidewire's tip as a ball in $\mathbb{R}^3$ with radius $r_g > 0$ and enforce a safety margin $d_m > 0$ from obstacles, resulting in $d_{min} = r_g + d_m$.

This step requires interactive placement of a suitable start configuration q_S for the instrument as well as a specific goal state q_G. Moreover, it includes the creation of transitions between neighboring labels: at the tricuspid valve between right atrium and ventricle, at the pulmonary valve between right ventricle and pulmonary artery and finally for SegThor at the aortic valve between aorta and left ventricle.

Motion Planning: We use a Bi-RRT with Bézier Splines as steering function [12] to search for collision-free trajectories. Computed paths interpolate between q_S and q_G while satisfying both constraints on distance and curvature. First, we

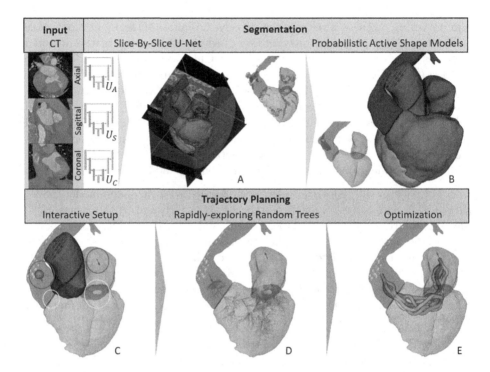

Fig. 2. Preoperative pipeline: a CT scan serves as input for 2D U-Nets to predict an initial segmentation (A). Probabilistic ASMs regularize the shapes of fragmented structures (B). A surgeon then interactively defines start and goal states (pink circles) and creates openings (yellow circles) (C). Bi-RRTs find feasible trajectories (D, search graphs in pink & cyan). Computed paths can be locally optimized using SCO (E). (Color figure online)

compute multiple solutions in a fixed time interval $T_{max} > 0$. Finally we perform SCO on each of these solutions to optimize with respect to a cost function weighing between clearance to obstacles and trajectory length [5].

3   Experiments

Source Code: C++ code of methods and experiments is publicly available on https://github.com/MECLabTUDA for the benefit of the research community.

Segmentation: We divided the two data sets (MMWHS, SegThor) into two subsets (first & second half) for twofold cross validation. U-Nets and PASMs were trained on one subset. Prediction and planning was performed on the other. For the two outputs $I^{\mathcal{U}}$ and $I^{\mathcal{P}}$ we computed Dice scores and Hausdorff distances.

Planning: We used all three sets $M^{GT}, M^{\mathcal{U}}, M^{\mathcal{P}}$ of surfaces meshes. First, the interactive setup of the preoperative pipeline (Step (C) in Fig. 2) was performed

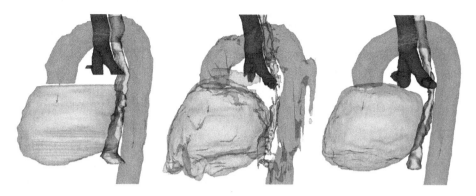

Fig. 3. Qualitative results on a SegThor sample (ground truth, U-Net & ours). Contrary to U-Net, our shape regularized approach provided shapes for feasible planning.

manually based on ground truth structures M^{GT}. For SegThor, start and goal states q_I, q_G were placed within the lower part of the descending and inferior to the ascending aorta (Fig. 1). For MMWHS, q_I, q_G were placed within the right atrium and the pulmonary artery. After setting up the motion planning definition, we computed access paths using the Bi-RRT three times in a row: Once using obstacles based on M^{GT}, once on $M^{\mathcal{U}}$ and once on $M^{\mathcal{P}}$, resulting in three sets of trajectories $T^{GT}, T^{\mathcal{U}}, T^{\mathcal{P}}$. We then measured the success rate for planning on both U-Net and PASM results, i.e. the percentage of data sets where at least one path was found for $T^{GT}, T^{\mathcal{U}}$ and $T^{\mathcal{P}}$. We then computed the distances to risk structures for $T^{GT}, T^{\mathcal{U}}, T^{\mathcal{P}}$ using only shapes M^{GT} as obstacles. This resulted in computing the true distance to risk structures when planning on U-Net and PASM, respectively. We then measured the mean distance of the minimum distances along each trajectory as well as the failure rate, i.e. the number of data sets were a path computed on segmentation results was actually below the critical safety distance d_{min}.

4   Results

SegTHOR: A functional evaluation of a preoperative pipeline evaluates both segmentation and planning metrics. Table 1 shows Dice and Hausdorff distances (HD) for esophagus, heart, trachea and aorta. While dice is comparable, our approach achieves for most anatomies significant improvement on Hausdorff distance. The qualitative example in Fig. 3 shows that a combination of fragmentation and isolated regions is often responsible for bad quality in the U-Net approach whereas our shape regularized solution provides realistic and accurate segmentation for planning. A downstream analysis on trajectory planning evaluates the overall quality and usefulness of the segmentation results by adding metrics on motion planning. Table 2 shows the success rate of the motion planning algorithm from Sect. 2. The fragmented structures from U-Net do not provide suitable obstacles for planning, whereas shape regularized meshes lead to

almost equal rates compared to ground truth planning. In successful cases, both
U-Net and our approach achieve slightly lower but still acceptable mean minimal
distances to risk structures due to the optimization step. The failure rate of 22%
should be addressed in future work.

Table 1. Results on Dice and HD with mean(SD) for SegTHOR and MMWHS.

	Dice		Hausdorff	
	U-Net	Ours	U-Net	Ours
Esophagus	0.46 (0.18)	**0.55 (0.18)**	23.91 (11.08)	**21.92 (8.97)**
Heart	0.90 (0.03)	0.91 (0.03)	37.05 (32.82)	**16.33 (5.18)**
Trachea	0.84 (0.09)	**0.87 (0.09)**	23.08 (11.62)	**19.19 (9.61)**
Aorta	0.80 (0.09)	**0.86 (0.08)**	26.46 (9.86)	**20.86 (9.68)**
Left ventricle	0.89 (0.07)	0.90 (0.07)	14.63 (10.99)	**8.56 (3.03)**
Right ventricle	0.86 (0.05)	0.86 (0.08)	23.05 (15.01)	**12.07 (5.80)**
Left atrium	0.91 (0.05)	0.90 (0.08)	17.67 (14.07)	**11.55 (6.26)**
Right atrium	0.86 (0.05)	**0.88 (0.05)**	23.30 (14.85)	**10.98 (3.16)**
Left myocardium	0.86 (0.05)	**0.88 (0.03)**	19.35 (15.96)	**9.62 (3.05)**
Ascending aorta	0.90 (0.20)	**0.92 (0.16)**	17.22 (12.31)	**14.82 (17.51)**
Pulmonary artery	0.83 (0.09)	0.83 (0.08)	32.80 (15.80)	**29.42 (15.52)**

Table 2. Quantitative results on planning metrics for SegThor and MMWHS.

	Success rate (%)		Mean safety distance (mm)		Failure rate (%)	
	SegThor	MMWHS	SegThor	MMWHS	SegThor	MMWHS
Ground-truth	98	100	4.70	4.39	–	–
U-Net	43	70	4.44	4.20	17	0
Ours	90	90	3.59	3.75	22	6

MMWHS: The evaluation on the MMWHS data set shows similar results. Table 1
again shows comparable Dice and Hausdorff scores clearly outperforming the
U-Net approach. Having the same success rate of 90% (Table 2) but an even
lower failure rate of 6% we conclude that shape regularization on deep learning
solutions provides a promising approach for future endovascular procedures.

5   Discussion and Conclusion

We propose a complete preoperative planning pipeline for endovascular procedures, performing successive steps of segmentation, interactive problem
definition and trajectory planning. Three key challenges - coherent boundaries

extraction, interactive setup and optimal trajectory planning- are addressed by shape regularization for segmentation, minimal interaction and finally RRTs followed by convex optimization. Our experiments use twofold cross validation on two publicly available data sets. Here, we show in a functional evaluation that uses both segmentation (Dice, Hausdorff) and planning metrics (success & failure rate) that in data-scarce environments this shape regularization provides adequate preoperative planning for endovascular procedures.

Future endovascular interventions should automatize complex procedures whereas key parts of the surgery remain in full control of the clinician. To reach this goal, we aim to further reduce the violation rate by improving on both segmentation and trajectory quality. Hybrid loss guided networks [6] might boost the performance of our U-Nets. The initialization of ASMs could then better capture the inferior part of the descending aorta (Fig. 3) or the transitions of the right ventricle to pulmonary artery and right atrium. For planning, we believe that trajectory optimization in a RRT*-like fashion [11] might be more robust leading to higher clearance and thus also to lower failure rates.

This paper takes a critical first step toward an extensive preoperative pipeline which would eventually save the surgeon from high accumulated radiation dose.

References

1. Burgner-Kahrs, J., Rucker, D.C., Choset, H.: Continuum robots for medical applications: a survey. IEEE Trans. Robot. **31**(6), 1261–1280 (2015)
2. Ganet, F., et al.: Development of a smart guide wire using an electrostrictive polymer: option for steerable orientation and force feedback. Sci. Rep. **5** (2015). Article number: 18593
3. Chi, W., et al.: Trajectory optimization of robot-assisted endovascular catheterization with reinforcement learning. In: 2018 IEEE/RSJ International Conference on Intelligent Robots and Systems (IROS), pp. 3875–3881, October 2018
4. Azizi, A., Tremblay, C., Martel, S.: Trajectory planning for vascular navigation from 3D angiography images and vessel centerline data. In: 2017 International Conference on Manipulation, Automation and Robotics at Small Scales (MARSS), pp. 1–6, July 2017
5. Fauser, J., Stenin, I., Kristin, J., Klenzner, T., Schipper, J., Mukhopadhyay, A.: Optimizing clearance of bézier spline trajectories for minimally-invasive surgery. In: Proceedings of the 22nd International Conference on Medical Image Computing and Computer-Assisted Intervention, MICCAI 2019, Shenzen, China, 13–17 October 2019. Springer, Cham (2019)
6. Petitjean, C.: Segmentation of THoracic Organs at Risk in CT images. In: Proceedings of the 2019 Challenge on Segmentation of THoracic Organs at Risk in CT Images (SegTHOR 2019), vol. 2348 (2019)
7. Fauser, J., et al.: Toward an automatic preoperative pipeline for image-guided temporal bone surgery. Int. J. Comput. Assist. Radiol. Surg. **14**(6), 967–976 (2019)
8. Tack, A., Mukhopadhyay, A., Zachow, S.: Knee menisci segmentation using convolutional neural networks: data from the osteoarthritis initiative. Osteoarthritis Cartilage **26**(5), 680–688 (2018)

9. Ronneberger, O., Fischer, P., Brox, T.: U-Net: convolutional networks for biomedical image segmentation. In: Navab, N., Hornegger, J., Wells, W.M., Frangi, A.F. (eds.) MICCAI 2015. LNCS, vol. 9351, pp. 234–241. Springer, Cham (2015). https://doi.org/10.1007/978-3-319-24574-4_28

10. Cootes, T., Taylor, C., Cooper, D., Graham, J.: Active shape models-their training and application. Comput. Vis. Image Underst. **61**(1), 38–59 (1995)

11. LaValle, S.M.: Planning Algorithms. Cambridge University Press, Cambridge (2006)

12. Fauser, J., Sakas, G., Mukhopadhyay, A.: Planning nonlinear access paths for temporal bone surgery. Int. J. Comput. Assist. Radiol. Surg. **13**(5), 637–646 (2018)

13. Schulman, J., et al.: Motion planning with sequential convex optimization and convex collision checking. Int. J. Robot. Res. **33**(9), 1251–1270 (2014)

14. Zhuang, X., et al.: Evaluation of algorithms for multi-modality whole heart segmentation: an open-access grand challenge. CoRR abs/1902.07880 (2019)

15. Valette, S., Chassery, J.M.: Approximated centroidal voronoi diagrams for uniform polygonal mesh coarsening. Comput. Graph. Forum **23**, 381–390 (2004)

16. Kirschner, M.: The probabilistic active shape model: from model construction to flexible medical image segmentation. Ph.D. thesis, TU Darmstadt (2013)

Guided Unsupervised Desmoking of Laparoscopic Images Using Cycle-Desmoke

V. Vishal[1], Neeraj Sharma[2], and Munendra Singh[1(✉)]

[1] Department of Mechatronics Engineering, Manipal Institute of Technology,
Manipal Academy of Higher Education, Manipal 576104, Karnataka, India
`vishalv7197@gmail.com`, `munendra107@gmail.com`
[2] School of Biomedical Engineering,
Indian Institute of Technology (Banaras Hindu University),
Varanasi 221005, India
`neeraj.bme@iitbhu.ac.in`

Abstract. The generation of smoke in laparoscopic surgery due to laser ablation and cauterization causes deterioration in the visual quality of the operative field. In order to reduce the effect of smoke, the present paper proposes an end-to-end network, called Cycle-Desmoke. The network enhances the CycleGAN framework by adoption of a new generator architecture and addition of new Guided-Unsharp Upsample loss in combination to adversarial and cycle-consistency loss. The Atrous Convolution Feature Extraction Module present in the encoder blocks of the generator helps distinguishing smoke by capturing features at multiple scales by the use of kernels with different receptive fields. Further, the use of Guided-Unsharp Upsample loss supervises the upsampling process of the feature maps and helps improve the contrast of the desmoked image. The network performs robust unsupervised Image-to-Image Translation from smoke domain to smoke-free domain. The public Cholec80 dataset is used to evaluate the performance of the proposed method. Quantitative and qualitative comparative analysis of the proposed method over the state-of-the-methods reveals the effectiveness of the method at the task of smoke removal and enhancement of the image.

Keywords: Smoke removal · Image enhancement · Laparoscopic surgery

1 Introduction

In laparoscopic surgery, the visualization of the operative field is of great utility for the surgeon as well as for the computer-assistive algorithms such as segmentation and detection of different tissues and surgical instruments. The generation of several artefacts such as noise, abrupt illumination changes, specular reflections and smoke in laparoscopic surgery degrades the quality of the visualization and

© Springer Nature Switzerland AG 2019
L. Zhou et al. (Eds.): OR 2.0 2019/MLCN 2019, LNCS 11796, pp. 21–28, 2019.
https://doi.org/10.1007/978-3-030-32695-1_3

hampers the efficiency of the surgeons and image-guided navigational systems. In this proposed work, we focus on the task of smoke removal in laparoscopy images using a computational, data driven approach. There exist several smoke evacuation techniques [1] that help to remove smoke but they rely on additional hardware instalments and have constraints. Our method directly works on the image data and helps improve the visualization by removing the smoke component and leads to enhancement of the image.

There exist several methods for the task of desmoking in laparoscopic images. Conventional methods represented the problem to be similar to dehazing, defogging and adopted the atmospheric scattering model to represent the phenomenon. He et al. [2] proposed a single image dehazing method using dark channel prior. The prior information utilized was based on the occurrence of some pixels in the local patches whose intensity are to be very low in at least one colour channel. In [3], Wang et al. assumed smoke to have low inter-channel and low contrast and proposed a variational method to estimate the smoke veil for desmoking. Although these methods led to enhancement of the image, they still lacked the ability to semantically distinguish and remove the smoke component in an image robustly. In recent times,several Deep learning methods have been proposed [5–8] for desmoking. Kotwal et al. [4] proposed a deep learning approach for desmoking on a synthetically generated dataset by transfer learning the task of smoke removal by using the AOD-Net. Wang et al. [7] performed desmoking by proposing a new Laplacian image pyramid decomposition input strategy on a synthetic dataset and evaluated the performance of the method on real smoke dataset. These new methods have outperformed the conventional methods by adopting the data-driven approach.

The proposed work focuses on translating a laparoscopy image from smoke domain to smoke-free domain. The method enhances the CycleGAN [9] framework used for unsupervised Image-to-Image Translation. The main contributions of the work are:

1. A new generator architecture that consists of Atrous Convolution Feature Extraction Module (ACFEM) at each encoder block, that helps to capture features at multiple scales by the use of kernels of different receptive fields. The upsampling operation is performed by means of pixel shuffle, leading to efficient transfer of the features in the network.

2. The use of unsharp images of the smoke images in the Guided-Unsharp Upsample loss in addition to the adversarial and cycle-consistency loss helps supervise the upsampling operation and also helps in contrast enhancement of the desmoked image.

3. The proposed end-to-end network performs unsupervised Image-to-Image translation from smoke to smoke-free domain in an unpaired manner without the need for synthetic ground truth data, hence removing the need for simulation to real-world domain adaptation.

2   Method

This section explains the loss function and network architectures of the generator and the discriminator. The Cycle-Desmoke framework is derived from the CycleGAN [9] framework. It consists of two generator networks G_S, G_{D_S} that generate synthetic smoke and desmoke images respectively and two discriminator network D_S and D_{D_S} that help to distinguish the synthetic smoke and desmoked images from the real smoke and smoke-free images respectively.

2.1   Guided-Unsharp Upsample Loss

The CycleGAN architecture utilizes the adversarial and cycle-consistency losses to perform unpaired image-to-image translation. The adversarial loss helps produce images of high perceptual quality by adopting a min-max optimization between the generator and discriminator networks. While, the cycle-consistency loss employs a *L1-norm* between the input and the reconstructed images to constrain the generated synthetic images to match the desired domain. Although these losses bring about image translation, they do not utilize the features information in the network. Hence, to guide the features in the network we introduce the Guided-Unsharp Upsample loss.

The upsampling operation helps realise desired dimensions for a feature map after the feature map has undergone reduction in spatial dimension after certain number of downsampling operations. In the proposed work, we utilize pixel shuffle to upsample the feature maps. A supervision for the upsampling operation is of great utility as it helps guide the network to accurately predict the desired image. This also helps in refinement of features in the upsampling operations. The unsharp masking technique helps increase the high frequency components and sharpens the images, highlighting fine details and edges. As smoke reduces the contrast of the image, unsharp masking works as a local contrast enhancement technique. The formulation of the technique is given as:

$$g(x,y) = f(x,y) - f_{smooth}(x,y) \tag{1}$$

$$f_{sharp}(x,y) = f(x,y) + k \times g(x,y) \tag{2}$$

Where $f(x,y)$ is the image, $f_{smooth}(x,y)$ is the image obtained after smoothing/blurring by convolution operation and $g(x,y)$ is the image that contains high frequency information. The $f_{sharp}(x,y)$ image is realised on adding original image with weighted $g(x,y)$ with amount k. The enhancement of contrast during the process desmoking helps reduce the low contrast smoke component. Hence, the comparison of unsharp images with the prediction from different decoder levels, help guide the upsampling process. This loss is applicable to the generator network responsible for desmoking. The loss is given as:

$$L_{GUU}(G_{DS}) = \sum_j ||Y_d - Y_{us}|| \tag{3}$$

where, Y_d and Y_{us} are the prediction and unsharp images at particular decoder block j.

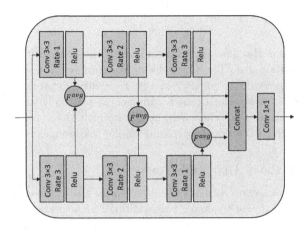

Fig. 1. Representation of Atrous Convolution Feature Extraction Module. The rate denotes the dilation rate of the convolution operation.

2.2 Aggregate Loss Function

The Cycle-Desmoke has an additional loss to the loss function in CycleGAN architecture. The loss function of CycleGAN is denoted as $L_{CycleGAN}(G_S, G_{DS}, D_S, D_{DS})$.

The complete loss function for training the framework is given as:

$$L(G_S, G_{DS}, D_S, D_{DS}) = L_{CycleGAN}(G_S, G_{DS}, D_S, D_{DS})+ \\ \alpha \times L_{GUU}(G_{DS}) \tag{4}$$

The term α controls the effect of the Guided-Unsharp Upsample loss.

2.3 Atrous Convolution Feature Extraction Module

The use of atrous convolutions to control the receptive field has resulted in remarkable results at tasks like semantic segmentation [10] and object detection [11]. The atrous convolutions allows to vary the dimension of the receptive field of the kernel without increasing the number of parameters as it pads zeros between kernel values. In context of the smoke removal problem, the occurrence of smoke can be either heterogeneous or homogeneous in the image, hence a robust feature extraction to capture features at multiple scales is essential. The Atrous Convolution Feature Extraction Module (ACFEM) employs a convolution 3×3 kernel with three different rates of dilation, i.e 1,2 and 3 and the receptive field of the atrous kernels match the dimension of 3×3, 5×5 and 7×7 kernels respectively. Figure 1, pictorially represents the flow of the feature maps across the different atrous convolutions. The flow of features across two branches, one with reducing receptive field and the other with increasing receptive field, helps in capturing a diverse set of features and the F_{avg}, average of the input feature maps helps to obtain the optimal features from both the branches. Convolution 1×1 kernel is

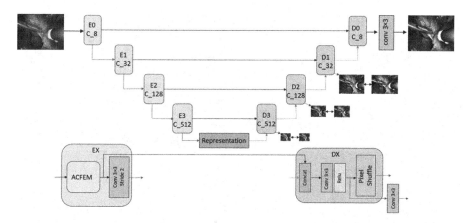

Fig. 2. The representation of the Generator network G_{DS} responsible for desmoking. G_S is similar to G_{DS} with the exception of the Guided-Unsharp Upsample loss setup

used to control the dimension of the output feature map. If the channel dimension of the input feature map is M, the atrous convolutions and convolution 1×1 kernel maintain the same channel depth and the output feature map has channel dimension of M. Hence, ACFEM helps in capturing features effective at distinguishing the smoke component in the image and performs efficient feature extraction.

2.4 Generator and Discriminator Networks

The generator network is represented in Fig. 2. It consists of an encoder-decoder structure. Each encoder block consists of Atrous Convolution Feature Extraction Module (ACFEM) and a 3×3 convolution with stride 2 to downsample the feature map by a factor of two. There exists four encoder blocks and a deep representation bottleneck followed by four decoder blocks. Corresponding encoder and decoder blocks are connected via skip connections. The feature map at a decoder block after convolution operation proceeds to pixel shuffle [12] for upsampling and convolution operation that outputs a prediction image that gets compared with the unsharp image at each decoder block except the last one.

The discriminator in CycleGAN [9] is utilized as the discriminator network for Cycle-Desmoke. The network utilizes 70×70 overlapping image patches to distinguish smoke images from smoke-free images.

3 Experimentation and Results

3.1 Dataset and Implementation Details

The dataset [13] used for the present study consists of 100K smoke/non-smoke images extracted from the Cholec80 dataset [14]. The training and test set consists of 1200 and 200 unpaired set of smoke and smoke-free images. The dimension of the image is maintained as 240×320 in order to remove the black corner

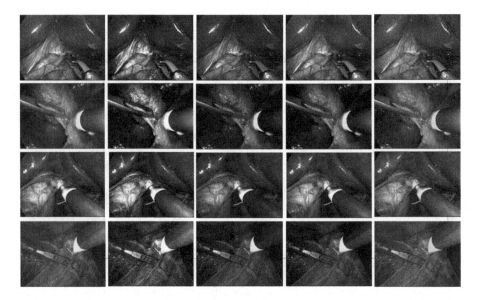

Fig. 3. Qualitative evaluation of smoke removal on randomly selected images from test set. First column: smoke images, second column: Non-Local Dehaze, third column: DCP, fourth column: DehazeNet, fifth column: Proposed method

details and enable the network to learn only the information in the operative field. The images in the smoke domain contains smoke of varying levels and depth and this ensures the network learns on different smoke levels.

The network is end-to-end trained with a learning rate of 0.0001 for the first 100 epochs and then the learning rate is linearly decayed to zero till 200 epochs. ADAM optimizer is used to optimize the generator and discriminator networks. The term α is set to 0.5 in the loss function. The convolution kernel dimension used for obtaining the unsharp images is 9×9 and the amount of sharpening i.e term k is set to 1.5. The tensorflow framework was used to train the network on a single NVidia Tesla T4 GPU.

3.2   Results

The qualitative and quantitative comparative analysis of the proposed Cycel-Desmoke is performed with state-of-the-art methods like Non-Local Dehaze [15], Dark channel prior (DCP) [2] and DehazeNet [16]. It is observed that the state-of-the-art methods although remove smoke to a certain extent, they lack the ability to maintain the colour consistency with respect to the smoke-free domain. The Non-Local Dehaze over saturates the color, causing difficulty in accurate differentiation of tissues. On the other hand, DCP seems to produce lower contrast images compared to the proposed method, while DehazeNet fails at removing smoke that is heterogeneous in nature. Hence, the lacking capabilities of other methods is efficiently handled by the proposed Cycle-Desmoke, that generates images with good contrast, colour consistency and robust smoke removal for both heterogeneous and homogeneous smoke (Fig. 3). The quantitative metrics used to denote the performance of smoke removal are, BRISQE [17]: Blind/Referenceless Image Spatial Quality Evaluator, PIQUE [18]: Perception-based Image QUality Evaluator, and CEIQ [19]: Quality Assessment of Contrast-Distorted Images. Lower values of BRISQE and PIQUE, higher values of CEIQ denote better image quality. It is evident from Table 1, that the proposed method obtains the best metric values and outperforms the other methods.

Table 1. Quantitative evaluation of smoke removal of other methods and the proposed method. The analysis has been performed on the test set. SD denotes Standard deviation

Method	Nonlocal Dehaze			DCP			DehazeNet			Proposed		
Image quality	BRISQE	PIQUE	CEIQ	BRISQE	PIQUE	CEIQ	BRISQE	PIQUE	CEIQ	BRISQE	PIQUE	CEIQ
Mean	19.06	36.18	3.15	20.95	32.54	2.95	21.07	33.78	3.15	17.71	25.71	3.29
SD	5.64	4.63	0.14	5.40	5.25	0.14	5.26	5.67	0.16	5.64	4.09	0.11

4 Conclusion

In this work, we proposed an end-to-end network called Cycle-Desmoke that relies on a new generator architecture that consists of Atrous Convolution Feature Extraction Module (ACFEM) that helped in alleviating the smoke component at multiple scales and ensures the performance is analogous for both heterogeneous and homogeneous smoke. The use of Guide-Unsharp Upsample loss in addition to the cycle-consistency and adversarial loss helped to enhance the contrast of the desmoked image and also recover fine details. The quantitative and qualitative analysis of proposed method with other state-of-the-art methods depicts considerable improvement in terms of smoke removal and image quality as well. This work focuses primarily on single-image desmoking, it would be advantageous to utilize the spatial-temporal relationship between each frame in the video sequence to supervise the network to perform smoke removal. Hence, having a digital solution to remove surgical smoke in laparoscopic surgery would not only prove beneficial for practitioners, surgeons but also help improve the efficiency of computer-assistive algorithms.

References

1. Takahashi, H., et al.: Automatic smoke evacuation in laparoscopic surgery: a simplified method for objective evaluation. Surg. Endosc. **27**(8), 2980–2987 (2013)
2. He, K., Sun, J., Tang, X.: Single image haze removal using dark channel prior. IEEE Trans. Pattern Anal. Mach. Intell. **33**(12), 2341–2353 (2010)
3. Wang, C., Cheikh, F.A., Kaaniche, M., Beghdadi, A., Elle, O.J.: Variational based smoke removal in laparoscopic images. Biomed. Eng. Online **17**(1), 139 (2018)

4. Kotwal, A., Bhalodia, R., Awate, S.P.: Joint desmoking and denoising of laparoscopy images. In: 2016 IEEE 13th International Symposium on Biomedical Imaging (ISBI), pp. 1050–1054. IEEE (2016)

5. Bolkar, S., Wang, C., Cheikh, F.A., Yildirim, S.: Deep smoke removal from minimally invasive surgery videos. In: 2018 25th IEEE International Conference on Image Processing (ICIP), pp. 3403–3407. IEEE (2018)

6. Sidorov, O., Wang, C., Cheikh, F.A.: Generative Smoke Removal. arXiv preprint arXiv:1902.00311 (2019)

7. Wang, C., Mohammed, A.K., Cheikh, F.A., Beghdadi, A., Elle, O.J.: Multiscale deep desmoking for laparoscopic surgery. In: Medical Imaging 2019: Image Processing, vol. 10949, p. 109491Y. International Society for Optics and Photonics (2019)

8. Chen, L., Tang, W., John, W.N.: Unsupervised learning of surgical smoke removal from simulation (2018)

9. Zhu, J.Y., Park, T., Isola, P., Efros, A.A.: Unpaired image-to-image translation using cycle-consistent adversarial networks. In: Proceedings of the IEEE International Conference on Computer Vision, pp. 2223–2232 (2017)

10. Chen, L.-C., Zhu, Y., Papandreou, G., Schroff, F., Adam, H.: Encoder-decoder with atrous separable convolution for semantic image segmentation. In: Ferrari, V., Hebert, M., Sminchisescu, C., Weiss, Y. (eds.) ECCV 2018. LNCS, vol. 11211, pp. 833–851. Springer, Cham (2018). https://doi.org/10.1007/978-3-030-01234-2_49

11. Guan, T., Zhu, H.: Atrous faster R-CNN for small scale object detection. In: 2017 2nd International Conference on Multimedia and Image Processing (ICMIP), pp. 16–21. IEEE (2017)

12. Shi, W., et al.: Real-time single image and video super-resolution using an efficient sub-pixel convolutional neural network. In: Proceedings of the IEEE Conference on Computer Vision and Pattern Recognition, pp. 1874–1883 (2016)

13. Leibetseder, A., Primus, M.J., Petscharnig, S., Schoeffmann, K.: Real-time image-based smoke detection in endoscopic videos. In: Proceedings of the on Thematic Workshops of ACM Multimedia 2017, pp. 296–304. ACM (2017)

14. Twinanda, A.P., Shehata, S., Mutter, D., Marescaux, J., De Mathelin, M., Padoy, N.: EndoNet: a deep architecture for recognition tasks on laparoscopic videos. IEEE Trans. Med. Imaging 36(1), 86–97 (2016)

15. Berman, D., Avidan, S.: Non-local image dehazing. In: Proceedings of the IEEE Conference on Computer Vision and Pattern Recognition, pp. 1674–1682 (2016)

16. Cai, B., Xu, X., Jia, K., Qing, C., Tao, D.: DehazeNet: an end-to-end system for single image haze removal. IEEE Trans. Image Process. 25(11), 5187–5198 (2016)

17. Mittal, A., Moorthy, A.K., Bovik, C.: No-reference image quality assessment in the spatial domain. IEEE Trans. Image Process. 21(12), 4695–4708 (2012)

18. Venkatanath, N., Praneeth, D., Bh, M.C., Channappayya, S.S., Medasani, S.S.: Blind image quality evaluation using perception based features. In: 2015 Twenty First National Conference on Communications (NCC), pp. 1–6. IEEE (2015)

19. Yan, J., Li, J., Fu, X.: No-reference quality assessment of contrast-distorted images using contrast enhancement. arXiv preprint arXiv:1904.08879 (2019)

Unsupervised Temporal Video Segmentation as an Auxiliary Task for Predicting the Remaining Surgery Duration

Dominik Rivoir[1,3]([✉]), Sebastian Bodenstedt[1], Felix von Bechtolsheim[2],
Marius Distler[2], Jürgen Weitz[2,3], and Stefanie Speidel[1,3]

[1] Translational Surgical Oncology,
National Center for Tumor Diseases (NCT), Dresden, Germany
{dominik.rivoir,sebastian.bodenstedt,stefanie.speidel}@nct-dresden.de
[2] Department of Visceral, Thoracic and Vascular Surgery,
Faculty of Medicine and University Hospital Carl Gustav Carus,
Technische Universität Dresden, Dresden, Germany
[3] Centre for Tactile Internet with Human-in-the-Loop (CeTI),
TU Dresden, Dresden, Germany

Abstract. Estimating the remaining surgery duration (RSD) during surgical procedures can be useful for OR planning and anesthesia dose estimation. With the recent success of deep learning-based methods in computer vision, several neural network approaches have been proposed for fully automatic RSD prediction based solely on visual data from the endoscopic camera. We investigate whether RSD prediction can be improved using unsupervised temporal video segmentation as an auxiliary learning task. As opposed to previous work, which presented supervised surgical phase recognition as auxiliary task, we avoid the need for manual annotations by proposing a similar but unsupervised learning objective which clusters video sequences into temporally coherent segments. In multiple experimental setups, results obtained by learning the auxiliary task are incorporated into a deep RSD model through feature extraction, pretraining or regularization. Further, we propose a novel loss function for RSD training which attempts to counteract unfavorable characteristics of the RSD ground truth. Using our unsupervised method as an auxiliary task for RSD training, we outperform other self-supervised methods and are comparable to the supervised state-of-the-art. Combined with the novel RSD loss, we slightly outperform the supervised approach.

Funded by the German Research Foundation (DFG, Deutsche Forschungsgemeinschaft) as part of Germany's Excellence Strategy – EXC 2050/1 – Project ID 390696704 – Cluster of Excellence "Centre for Tactile Internet with Human-in-the-Loop" (CeTI) of Technische Universität Dresden.

© Springer Nature Switzerland AG 2019
L. Zhou et al. (Eds.): OR 2.0 2019/MLCN 2019, LNCS 11796, pp. 29–37, 2019.
https://doi.org/10.1007/978-3-030-32695-1_4

Keywords: Unsupervised learning · Representation learning ·
Remaining surgery duration · Temporal segmentation ·
Computer-assisted surgery

1   Introduction

Resources in the operating room (OR) are among the most expensive in a hospital and careful OR planning is crucial in order to minimize waiting times and idle phases. Estimating the remaining surgery duration (RSD) at specified points during an intervention can facilitate more efficient utilization of OR resources.

This work builds on deep learning-based methods for fully automated RSD prediction based solely on endoscopic video data [1,2,10]. Since the remaining time for each frame can be inferred automatically from a given videos, RSD prediction is a self-supervised task. This property is especially useful in medical applications, where manually annotating data is expensive.

However, RSD prediction is an extremely challenging task due to the complexity and uniqueness of a surgical procedure. It appears to require a high-level understanding of the workflow and progress of the surgery. These factors probably contribute to RSD models tending to overfit without proper regularization or pretraining [10]. To alleviate this problem, Twinanda et al. propose an RSD prediction network which is encouraged to learn progress-related features and utilizes the elapsed time in addition to visual features [10]. Bodenstedt et al. use multimodal sensor data from the OR including visual data and tool signals for their prediction [2]. State-of-the-art results are obtained by Aksamentov et al. who suggest to pretrain the RSD model on surgical phase recognition as an auxiliary task [1]. However, surgical phase recognition is a supervised task and therefore reduces the advantages of self-supervised RSD training.

Our contributions consist of proposing an unsupervised auxiliary task to improve RSD prediction, namely unsupervised temporal video segmentation. To solve the auxiliary task, we present a method for finding segmentations that capture the progress of a surgery similar to surgical phases but without the need for manual annotations. As indicated in [1,10], progress-related features can be beneficial for RSD prediction. Using an unsupervised auxiliary task makes this approach widely applicable to different datasets. Several image-based unsupervised temporal video segmentation methods have been proposed [6–8]. We adopt the method from [7] since its iterative procedure allows us to learn task-related image features. The other approaches extract or learn features prior to segmentation, making them unsuitable as an auxiliary task. Finally, we propose a novel loss function that targets undesirable characteristics of the RSD ground truth.

2   Methods

Our approach combines models for RSD prediction and unsupervised temporal video segmentation. A model consisting of a Convolutional Neural Network (CNN) for visual feature extraction and a Long Short-Term Memory network

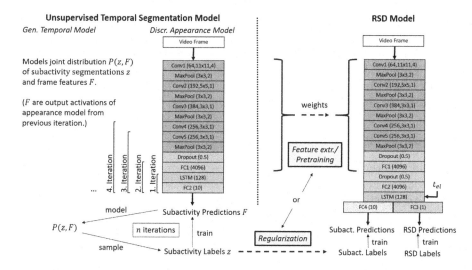

Fig. 1. Summary of the proposed learning pipelines. Step 1: train the unsupervised temporal segmentation model for n iterations. Step 2: either use the learned weights for feature extraction or pretraining or the learned segmentation labels for regularization. Note that $FC4$ only exists in the regularization pipeline. Network layer notation: convolutional layers $Conv*$ *(filter size, kernel size, stride)*, max-pooling layers *MaxPool (kernel size, stride)*, dropout layers *Dropout (drop probability)* and fully-connected and recurrent layers $FC*/LSTM$ *(size)*.

(LSTM) for propagating information through time is trained to perform our main task, RSD prediction, similar to [1, 2, 10]. For the temporal segmentation task, we use an unsupervised approach to train a discriminative-generative model alternating between learning segmentation labels through a generative model and learning visual features in a discriminative CNN-LSTM network. The results obtained by solving the temporal segmentation task can be leveraged for RSD prediction in several ways. First, we assume that the temporal segmentation training encourages the CNN-LSTM model to learn features relevant for RSD prediction. Thus, we investigate reusing the learned feature representations by initializing the CNN-LSTM model for RSD prediction with the learned network weights. We then pursue two different strategies for further training the RSD model: we either finetune only the upper layers or none of the layers in the CNN. In a complementary approach, we use the obtained segment labels to formulate an additional objective to regularize the RSD model during training.

2.1 RSD Model

For our RSD model (Fig. 1, right), we use an AlexNet-style CNN [5] to extract visual features from the video frames of a recorded surgical procedure. The feature representations are concatenated with the elapsed time t_{el} of the procedure and fed into an LSTM, similar to [10]. The LSTM can consider features from the current and previous frames and produces an RSD estimate for each frame of the video. The network predicts the remaining duration in minutes, scaled by a factor of 0.05 due to high values of up to 100 min. RSD prediction is formulated as a regression task and optimized according to the SmoothL1 loss [10]. We use a simpler model instead of *RSDNet* [10], since the latter showed no empirical improvement in combination with our auxiliary task.

2.2   Unsupervised Temporal Video Segmentation Model

We extend a method from [7] for recognition and segmentation of complex activities in videos, i.e. activities consisting of several subactivities. The author's definiton of a complex activity can be applied to surgeries, where subactivities could represent surgical phases or similar steps.

The unsupervised learning algorithm alternates between learning frame features and subactivity labels (Fig. 2). Given the current subactivity labels, a discriminative appearance model learns frame features in a supervised manner. A generative temporal model is then estimated, which models the distribution of subactivity lengths and subactivity orders, given the distribution of frames in the learned appearance space. The subactivity lengths and order determine the segmentation of a video. After sampling new lengths and orders and subsequently updating subactivity labels, the algorithm continues to learn new frame features.

The discriminative appearance model is a CNN-LSTM model (Fig. 1, left) optimized via the cross-entropy loss. An extensive hyperparameter search suggested the use of ten subactivities. Opposed to our deep learning approach, the appearance model in the original paper [7] learns a simple linear embedding of image features. When replacing this simple model by a complex CNN-LSTM model, care must be taken to avoid overfitting on unrefined segmentations from early iterations. To this end, only the top two layers of the network are optimized in the first iteration and layers are added incrementally after each iteration (Fig. 1, left). In turn, the incremental depth increase requires an initialization of the fixed layers. We pretrain the CNN using the 2nd-order temporal coherence objective [4], which has shown promising results on a similar task [3].

The generative temporal model estimates the joint distribution of frame features and subactivity segmentations. The distribution over segmentations is modeled by distributions over the length of each subactivity *(Multinomial)* and over the order of subactivities *(Generalized Mallows Model)*. Sampling-based approximations are used to infer segmentations. The generative temporal model is almost identical to the one proposed in [7]. We only drop background model.

The method produces new models after each iteration. Hence, we need to evaluate and select a model to use as a support for the RSD model. Since the ground truth segmentation labels are unknown, we require a surrogate quality measure. We define a measure TC which quantifies the temporal coherence of subacitivty predictions by the appearance model. More precisely, we measure the prediction's accuracy with respect to the best match of coherent segmentations with the same subacitivity lengths. This measure intends to capture how well

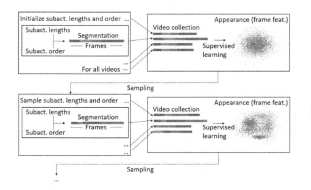

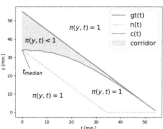

Fig. 2. The unsupervised temporal segmentation method adopted from [7]. We alternate between learning frame features and subactivity labels.

Fig. 3. Ground truth $gt(t)$, corridor border $c(t)$ and median-based prediction $n(t)$ for one surgery.

a model has learned progress-related features. Preliminary experiments showed that the measure selects models which are beneficial for RSD prediction.

2.3   Combined Learning Pipelines

Figure 1 shows three strategies for combining models.

Feature Extraction: The unsupervised temporal segmentation method is used to train the CNN-LSTM network of the discriminative appearance model. The weights learned from layers *Conv1* to *FC1* are then re-used for the RSD model. While training the RSD model, the initialized layers are fixed. Only layers *FC2*, *LSTM* and *FC3* are optimized. This method is equivalent to feature extraction, where layers *Conv1* to *FC1* serve as a feature extractor for a shallow RSD model.

Pretraining: Pretraining is almost identical to feature extraction, except that the layers *Conv5* and *FC1* are optimized during RSD training after being initialized by the temporal segmentation method. In order to prevent the previously learned information from being overwritten too quickly, a lower learning rate is applied to pretrained layers. To summarize, layers *Conv1* to *Conv4* are fixed, *Conv5* and *FC1* are optimized with a low learning rate, and *FC2*, *LSTM* and *FC3* are optimized using the regular learning rate.

Regularization: The resulting subactivity labels of a learned temporal segmentation model are re-used for supervision during RSD training. First, segmentations are learned for each video by the unsupervised temporal segmentation model. Then, the RSD model is jointly trained on RSD prediction and predicting the current subactivity according to the previously found segmentations.

2.4 Corridor-Based RSD Loss Function

In the early stages of a procedure it is extremely challenging to correctly predict the remaining duration since later occurring events are not yet known. To
account for this, we propose an alternative RSD loss function which reduces the
influence of early errors. Intuitively, we do not want to penalize the best guess at
the beginning of a procedure, which is the average length of the given procedure
type. For each video, we therefore define an area between the ground truth $gt(t)$
over time and a naïve median-based prediction $n(t) = max(t_{median} - t, 0)$, where
t_{median} is the median duration of all procedures in the training set. Errors within
this corridor are decreased by a weighting function π (Fig. 3). The corridor border $c(t) = \alpha_t g(t) + (1 - \alpha_t)n(t)$ is a linear combination of the ground truth $gt(t)$
and the median-based prediction $n(t)$.

Here $\alpha_t = 1 - \frac{2}{1+e^{5 \cdot prog(t)}}$ is a time-dependent linear factor similar to the
tanh function, where $prog(t) = \frac{t}{gt(t)+t}$ is the progress of the surgery in percent.
Intuitively, $c(t)$ is closer to the median-based prediction $n(t)$ at early time points,
when little information is available, and approaches the ground truth $gt(t)$ as
the procedure progresses. The weight $\pi(y, t)$ for a prediction y at time t is given
by

$$\pi(y, t) = \begin{cases} \left(\frac{|y-gt(t)|}{|c(t)-gt(t)|}\right)^2, & \text{if } c(t) \leq y \leq gt(t) \text{ or } gt(t) \leq y \leq c(t) \\ 1, & \text{otherwise} \end{cases} \quad (1)$$

π realizes a smooth weighting distribution along the y-axis inside the corridor
from $y = gt(t)$ to $y = c(t)$ (with $\pi(gt(t), t) = 0$ to $\pi(c(t), t) = 1$). For predictions
y outside the corridor, $\pi(y, t) = 1$. The corridor-weighted loss is finally given by

$$CorrSmoothL1(y, t) = \pi(y, t) \cdot SmoothL1(y, gt(t)) \quad (2)$$

3 Evaluation

We evaluate our proposed models on the publicly available Cholec80 dataset [9].
We use 50 videos for training, 10 for validation and 20 for testing. Video frames
are extracted at 1fps. We train the RSD models using the Adam optimizer (200
epochs, learning rate 10^{-5}, batch size 384, $\mathcal{L}_2$-weight 10^{-5}). For the pretraining
pipelines, we use SGD, run 250 epochs and update pretrained layers with a
learning rate of 10^{-6} since these settings empirically perform better. The other
settings are kept. For the segmentation model, Adam, learning rate 10^{-5}, batch
size 384, 5 epochs per iteration, 8 iterations, $\mathcal{L}_2$-weight 10^{-4} are used. We select
the best model from iterations 6 to 8 according to our TC measure (Sect. 2.2).

3.1 Baselines

We consider four baselines for RSD prediction: The simplest baseline is the RSD
model from Sect. 2.1 trained only on single-task RSD prediction with no auxiliary task *(None)*. The other baselines are supported by auxiliary tasks each

using all three proposed pipelines from Sect. 2.3. The first auxiliary task is temporal segmentation into 10 uniform segments *(Uniform)*. This is an interesting baseline that can provide insight into how much RSD-relevant information is gained by learning more refined segmentations. The other two auxiliary tasks are state-of-the-art approaches, namely supervised surgical phase recognition *(Phase)* [1] and self-supervised prediction of progress $prog(t)$ *(Progress)* reimplemented from [11], which is an updated version of the RSDNet from [10]. For the phase approach, we use the regularized RSD model from Fig. 1 in order preserve compariability to our methods. The main differences to the architecture from [1] are that we use an AlexNet-style CNN like in [11] and that we incorporate the elapsed time into the prediction like in [10, 11]. Hyperparameters of the optimization are identical to the proposed methods.

3.2   Results

Table 1 shows the mean average error (MAE) in minutes for each of our proposed models as well as all baselines using the SmoothL1 loss. All experiments involving our proposed method are performed four times, averaged and indicated by a standard deviation. Baseline experiments for settings which were effective for our method are repeated four times, in order to obtain more significant results.

Comparing our proposed methods, feature extraction achieves the best results (9.0 ± 0.1 min. MAE), while pretraining performs worst (9.3 ± 0.2) and high variances were observed during regularization (9.2 ± 0.5). The high expressivity of RSD models likely causes overfitting in the two latter setups. In the pretraining setting, the RSD model is the least expressive, as only the top layers are optimized after initialization by the segmentation method. Hence, it is supposedly less prone to overfitting. We also observe that our approach outperforms or matches the self-supervised approaches (single-task RSD, uniform segmentation and progress) for all learning pipelines. Using feature extraction, we even achieve results comparable to the supervised phase-based approach (9.0 vs. 8.9).

Next, we compare the CorrSmoothL1 loss to SmoothL1 on the previously most successful feature extraction and the regularization pipeline (Table 2), since the high variance in regularization experiments indicates potential for improvement. The first two result columns show RSD errors for both loss functions on the feature extraction pipeline. No clear difference can be observed. The single-task RSD model as well as most regularized models, however, improve drastically. Since CorrSmoothL1 aims to reduce overfitting, it is more effective on very expressive deep models such as the regularization models or the single-task model. In the feature extraction setup, which has significantly fewer trained parameters during RSD training, the model's low expressivity probably prevents further improvement. Using regularization, our approach improves from 9.2 to 8.7 min MAE and therefore exceeds our previously best result as well as all baselines. We even outperform all supervised phase-based setups. It is not clear how significant this difference is, since the supervised approach performed slightly better than ours in the SmoothL1 setup. However, even comparable results are

Table 1. Mean average error (MAE) in minutes for our proposed RSD models as well as state-of-the-art baselines.

Auxiliary task	Feature extraction	Pretraining	Regularization
Unsup. temp. seg. *(ours)*	9.0 (±0.1)	9.3 (±0.2)	9.2 (±0.5)
None	9.7 (±0.1)		
Uniform	9.4	9.4	9.4
Progress	9.0 (±0.1)	9.5	9.6
Phase *(supervised)*	**8.9** (±0.1)	**8.9**	9.1

Table 2. Comparison of RSD loss functions on the feature extraction and regularization pipelines. *In *None*, columns 2 and 4 as well as 3 and 5 refer to the same experiments.

Auxiliary task	Feature extraction		Regularization	
	SmoothL1	CorrSmoothL1	SmoothL1	CorrSmoothL1
Unsup. temp. seg. *(ours)*	9.0 (±0.1)	9.1 (±0.2)	9.2 (±0.5)	**8.7** (±0.2)
None*	9.7 (±0.1)	9.1 (±0.5)	9.7 (±0.1)	9.1 (±0.5)
Uniform	9.4	9.3	9.4	9.4
Progress	9.0 (±0.1)	9.1	9.6	9.2 (±0.4)
Phase *(supervised)*	8.9 (±0.1)	9.0	9.1	8.9 (±0.1)

very promising and our approach performs at least on a similar level as supervised methods. Figure 4 shows that subactivity labels corresponds fairly well to surgical phases but are more fine grained due to the higher number of segments. Using a hand-picked mapping from subactivities to phases, we achieve an accuracy of 71% and 72% on the training and test set for surgical phase recognition. A limitation of our proposed method remains the complexity of the whole model and achieving stable results poses a challenge.

Fig. 4. Ground truth of surgical phases and learned subactivities of exemplary training videos. Different shades illustrate how several subactivities correlate with one phase or vice versa. Our method does not provide a mapping from subactivities to phases.

4   Conclusion

We present unsupervised temporal video segmentation as a novel auxiliary task for video-based RSD prediction and propose three different learning pipelines to utilize unsupervised temporal segmentation learning for RSD modeling. In our experiments on the Cholec80 dataset, our approach compares favorably with self-supervised auxiliary tasks and performs comparably to the state of the art, which utilizes supervised surgical phase recognition as auxiliary task. This is very promising since the method does not require any manual annotations and therefore has potential for improvement by utilizing larger, unlabeled datasets. Further, we specifically target the problem that RSD ground truth labels can be misleading in early stages of a procedure. Our novel corridor-based loss shows clear improvements on deep RSD models. Using the corridor-based loss, we even outperform the state of the art when we regularize the RSD model with the unsupervised temporal segmentation task. Future work could evaluate our method on procedure types with higher variance in duration and therefore lower correlation between RSD and progress. Analyzing how our method transfers to these procedures is interesting since temporal segmentations can potentially model more complex temporal structures than progress. Also, the similarity of unsupervised segmentations and surgical phases induces interesting new research directions.

References

1. Aksamentov, I., Twinanda, A.P., Mutter, D., Marescaux, J., Padoy, N.: Deep neural networks predict remaining surgery duration from cholecystectomy videos. In: Descoteaux, M., Maier-Hein, L., Franz, A., Jannin, P., Collins, D.L., Duchesne, S. (eds.) MICCAI 2017. LNCS, vol. 10434, pp. 586–593. Springer, Cham (2017). https://doi.org/10.1007/978-3-319-66185-8_66
2. Bodenstedt, S., Wagner, M., Mündermann, L., Kenngott, H., Müller-Stich, B., et al.: Prediction of laparoscopic procedure duration using unlabeled, multimodal sensor data. IJCARS **14**(6), 1089–1095 (2019)
3. Funke, I., Jenke, A., Mees, S.T., Weitz, J., Speidel, S., Bodenstedt, S.: Temporal coherence-based self-supervised learning for laparoscopic workflow analysis. In: Stoyanov, D., et al. (eds.) CARE/CLIP/OR 2.0/ISIC -2018. LNCS, vol. 11041, pp. 85–93. Springer, Cham (2018). https://doi.org/10.1007/978-3-030-01201-4_11
4. Jayaraman, D., Grauman, K.: Slow and steady feature analysis: higher order temporal coherence in video. In: Proceedings of CVPR, pp. 3852–3861 (2016)
5. Krizhevsky, A., Sutskever, I., Hinton, G.E.: ImageNet classification with deep convolutional neural networks. In: NIPS, vol. 1 (2012)
6. Kukleva, A., Kuehne, H., Sener, F., Gall, J.: Unsupervised learning of action classes with continuous temporal embedding. In: Proceedings of CVPR, pp. 12066–12074 (2019)
7. Sener, F., Yao, A.: Unsupervised learning and segmentation of complex activities from video. In: CVPR, June 2018
8. Tran, D.T., Sakurai, R., Yamazoe, H., Lee, J.H.: Phase segmentation methods for an automatic surgical workflow analysis. IJBI (2017)
9. Twinanda, A.P., Shehata, S., Mutter, D., Marescaux, J., De Mathelin, M., Padoy, N.: EndoNet: a deep architecture for recognition tasks on laparoscopic videos. IEEE Trans. Med. Imaging **36**(1), 86–97 (2016)
10. Twinanda, A.P., Yengera, G., Mutter, D., Marescaux, J., Padoy, N.: RSDNet: learning to predict remaining surgery duration from laparoscopic videos without manual annotations. IEEE Trans. Med. Imaging **38**(4), 1069–1078 (2018)
11. Yengera, G., Mutter, D., Marescaux, J., Padoy, N.: Less is more: surgical phase recognition with less annotations through self-supervised pre-training of CNN-LSTM networks. arXiv preprint arXiv:1805.08569 (2018)

Live Monitoring of Haemodynamic Changes with Multispectral Image Analysis

Leonardo A. Ayala[1(✉)], Sebastian J. Wirkert[1], Janek Gröhl[1,2],
Mildred A. Herrera[3], Adrian Hernandez-Aguilera[3], Anant Vemuri[1],
Edgar Santos[3], and Lena Maier-Hein[1,2(✉)]

[1] Division Computer Assisted Medical Interventions (CAMI),
German Cancer Research Center (DKFZ), Heidelberg, Germany
{l.menjivar,l.maier-hein}@dkfz.de
[2] Medical Faculty, University of Heidelberg, Heidelberg, Germany
[3] Department of Neurosurgery, Heidelberg University Hospital, Heidelberg,
Germany

Abstract. State-of-the-art concepts in the field of computer assisted
medical interventions are typically based on registering pre-operative
imaging data to the patient. While this approach has many relevant clinical applications, it suffers from one core bottleneck: it cannot account for
tissue dynamics because it works with "offline" data. To overcome this
issue, we propose a new approach to surgical imaging that combines the
power of multispectral imaging with the speed and robustness of deep
learning based image analysis. Core innovation is an end-to-end deep
learning architecture that integrates all preprocessing steps as well as
the actual regression task in a single network. According to a quantitative *in silico* validation, our approach is well-suited for solving the inverse
problem of relating multispectral image pixels to underlying functional
tissue properties in real time. A porcine study further suggests that our
method is capable of monitoring haemodynamic changes *in vivo*. Deep
learning based multispectral imaging could thus become a valuable tool
for imaging tissue dynamics.

1 Introduction

A modality suitable for surgical imaging should provide real-time discrimination
of local tissue with a high contrast-to-noise-ratio (CNR) and spatio-temporal
context for global orientation and instrument guidance. It should ideally be
radiation-free and facilitate integration into the clinical workflow, in addition
to featuring a compact design at a low cost for a wide range of applicability
and acceptance. Unfortunately, none of the imaging modalities widely used at

The original version of this chapter was previously published non-open access. A Correction to this chapter is available at https://doi.org/10.1007/978-3-030-32695-1_13

Supplementary Information The online version contains supplementary material
available at https://doi.org/10.1007/978-3-030-32695-1_5.

© The Author(s) 2019, corrected publication 2024
L. Zhou et al. (Eds.): OR 2.0 2019/MLCN 2019, LNCS 11796, pp. 38–46, 2019.
https://doi.org/10.1007/978-3-030-32695-1_5

a clinical level meet all of these requirements. The field of computer assisted interventions addresses this bottleneck by registering 3D medical image data sets to the current patient anatomy for augmented reality visualization of subsurface anatomical details overlaid onto endoscopic video data, for example. One of the major bottlenecks of this approach, however, is that it is not well-suited for handling tissue dynamics. In particular, important information related to tissue perfusion or oxygenation (e.g. to detect ischemia) cannot be extracted from images acquired before the procedure.

The field of biophotonics refers to techniques that analyze light tissue interactions. In particular, multispectral (optical) imaging (MSI) has recently been used in biomedical engineering applications [1,6,14,15]. It takes advantage of the fact that different tissue components feature unique optical properties for each wavelength. As a consequence, the spectral profile contains information about the molecular composition of tissue, such as concentration of oxygenated and deoxygenated hemoglobin. Although recent research results are extremely encouraging, existing methods including recently emerging commercial solutions still suffer from two main drawbacks. (1) Speed: Most methods are not able to provide "live" augmented images, capable of giving immediate feedback to the surgeon. (2) Accuracy: Many methods have a lack of accuracy in the functional information conveyed by the images. This can be attributed to the fact that most systems for interventional *in vivo* multispectral imaging use linear estimation approaches based on the modified Beer-Lambert law, as described in [10]. While these methods are typically fast, they require small multispectral bandwidths, and they also rely on a number of unrealistic assumptions regarding tissue composition that potentially lead to imprecise results.

In this work, we build upon prior work of Wirkert et al. [14,15]. Here, the hypothesis was that machine learning based regression may address the issues currently faced by the community. The absence of a quantitative reference for the functional parameters (a requirement for training machine learning techniques) is overcome by a Monte Carlo simulation-based approach to regressor training. While the authors achieved high accuracy *in silico* in their previous work, their random forest (RF) implementation did not achieve real-time performance. One reason for this was that the image processing pipeline was relatively complex with several preprocessing steps before the RF regression. The purpose of this work was therefore to explore the use of deep learning for real-time estimation of functional parameters. The primary contributions are:

1. We present a deep learning based approach to real-time functional tissue parameter estimation with multispectral imaging. Core innovation is an end-to-end deep learning architecture that elegantly integrates all preprocessing steps as well as the actual regression task in a single network.
2. We demonstrate *in vivo* that our method is capable of monitoring haemodynamic changes in the brain. More specifically, we show that the changes in tissue oxygenation resulting from a phenomenon called spreading depolarization can be detected with our approach.

2   Methods

In this section we present our hardware setup (Sect. 2.1) as well as the computational methods for monitoring functional tissue parameters with an MSI camera (Sect. 2.2).

2.1   Multispectral Imaging Hardware

We use a Pixelteq camera (Largo, FL, USA) 5MPix Spectrocam which records multispectral images at a frame rate of 2 Hz. The central wavelengths of the eight filters were determined with the method described by Wirkert et. al. [13] and set to 470, 480, 511, 560, 580, 600, 660 and 700 nm. All bands have a full witdth at half maximum (FWHM) of 20 nm except for the 480 nm band which has a FWHM of 25 nm (by camera design). Recording of one MSI image at resolution 2058×2456 takes 400 ms. For illumination we use a standard surgical Xenon (Storz D-light P) light source.

2.2   End-to-End Deep Learning Pipeline for Multispectral Image Analysis

Our approach is based on the following hypotheses: (1) When applied to MSI data, machine learning based algorithms are better suited for solving the inverse problem of relating spectra to underlying tissue parameters than competing model-based approaches. (2) It is beneficial to train on individual pixels rather than whole images to facilitate the generation of realistic training data. (3) Compared to competing machine learning based approaches, deep learning based methods have higher potential to maximize both accuracy and speed. As shown in Fig. 1, our method involves two different networks with fully convolutional architectures. The training network learns the functional property estimation based on the simulated training data. Its weights and biases are transferred into the live validation network, which runs in a highly accelerated environment. One of the main advantages of our live validation network over other state-of-the-art methods is that the necessary data preprocessing steps are integrated into the network and can efficiently be performed on the Graphics Processing Unit (GPU, cf. Fig. 1).

Training Data Simulation. To simulate reflectance spectra as training data we use a generalized multi-layered tissue model as presented in [14,15]. For simulation of light transport we use the GPU accelerated Monte Carlo Multi Layer (GPU-MCML) software [2]. By default, we use 10^6 photons per simulation in the wavelenth range from 300–1000 nm with a stepsize of 2 nm and simulate a total of $500,000$ samples for training and $50,000$ samples for testing. Each layer comprises distinct values for blood volume fraction v_{hb}, reduced scattering coefficient at 500 nm a_{mie}, scattering power b_{mie}, anisotropy g, refractive index n and layer thickness d. In contrast to this, blood oxygenation sO_2 is kept constant across layers. The values for these parameters are uniformly drawn from the ranges detailed in [15]. From these values we calculate the wavelength dependent optical absorption μ_a and scattering μ_s as $\mu_a(\lambda) = v_{\text{hb}}(sO_2 \cdot \mu_{a_{\text{HbO2}}} + (1 - sO_2) \cdot$

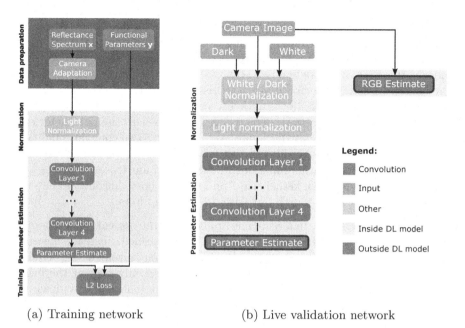

(a) Training network   (b) Live validation network

Fig. 1. Deep learning architecture for multispectral image analysis. (a) The network used for training, whose model parameters are re-used for the live validation network. (b) The live validation network used during the intervention, yielding the physiological parameters and RGB estimates. The estimated RGB image is only used for visualization.

$\mu_{a_{\mathrm{Hb}}}$) and $\mu_s(\lambda) = \frac{a_{mie}}{1-g}(\frac{\lambda}{500\,\mathrm{nm}})^{-b_{mie}}$. Where $\mu_{a_{\mathrm{HbO2}}}$ and $\mu_{a_{\mathrm{Hb}}}$ are the absorption coefficients of oxygenated and deoxygenated blood with the assumption of $150\,\mathrm{g}$ hemoglobin per liter blood and a_{mie}, b_{mie} are the scattering coefficient and scattering power respectively.

Preprocessing of Training Data. The spectral reflectance is an intrinsic property of tissue, independent of the imaging system employed. Nonetheless, recorded reflectances are heavily influenced by imaging system parts such as camera filter responses, camera quantum efficiency, and relative irradiance of light source. Hence, an important step in our processing pipeline is to transform simulated spectra into data that resembles measurements from our hardware setup as closely as possible. To achieve this, quantum efficiency provided by the manufacturer is used. We further acquired spectrometer (Ocean Optics HR2000+, Largo, Florida, USA) measurements of the camera filter transmission and light source relative irradiance. We use these measurements to transform our simulated spectra into a camera specific normalized reflectance space as described in [15] and referred to as "Camera Adaptation" in Fig. 1.

In a real scenario, recordings can be affected by changes in illumination such as illumination intensity and distance of light source to the imaged region. In order to reduce this effect, a light normalization step is introduced in the network, as depicted in Fig. 1. This step is computed on the GPU and comprises normalizing the spectra with its L_1 norm, the same normalization is then implemented in the *in vivo* network. In order to take into account possible tissue homogeneities that can arise in a real scenario, every reflectance training sample is augmented to match a region of 3×3 pixels and multiplicative noise model of 20% signal to noise ratio (SNR) is added to each pixel.

We then trained the network depicted in Fig. 1a, where the parameter estimation block consists of 5 convolutional layers. The first two convolutional layer are composed of 50 learnable filters with kernel size 2 and in place Rectified Linear Unit (ReLU) activation functions, the third and fourth convolutions have the same structure but with kernel size 1 and the last convolution has the same structure as the third and fourth but with 2 learnable filters.

Real-Time Application. In a real-time application, the optical system domain adaptation described in the previous section is not needed. Instead, measurements of a white reference standard and a dark field measurement are required for the light source normalization. This step is required only once at the beginning of the recordings. As these preprocessing steps potentially slow down the regression process, they are incorporated directly into the real-time deep learning network and implemented on the GPU (cf. Fig. 1b).

To apply our method, we copy the weights and biases of our trained network into the corresponding module of the real-time validation network. White (W) and dark (D) recordings of a standard reference (Spectralon) are included directly into the network, as illustrated in Fig. 1. Each MSI recording is then normalized as follows: $R = \frac{I-D}{W-D}$ where I represents the raw MSI image and R the normalized image. Furthermore, the L_1 normalization described in Sect. 2.2 is implemented as part of the deep learning framework.

3   Experiments and Results

Our validation of the proposed method for functional tissue parameter estimation from MSI comprised two studies: a quantitative *in silico* study and an *in vivo* feasibility experiment. The purpose of the *in silico* validation was to compare the performance of our approach to state-of-the-art RF regression by estimating blood oxygenation on a held out test set. Here, we used the median absolute error of sO_2, which we calculate as $e_{\mathrm{abs}}^{sO_2} = \left| s\hat{O}_2 - sO_2^{\mathrm{GT}} \right|$, the interquartile range of the sO_2 absolute error and regression speed as our target metrics. The purpose of the *in vivo* experiment was to investigate whether we can detect haemodynamic changes on porcine brain images when we apply the network on data recorded with the multispectral imaging hardware described in Sect. 2.1.

3.1   *In Silico* Quantitative Validation

We compared our method to RF-based inference [14,15] as a reference method on the exact same data set used previously [15] (500,000 training cases and 50,000 test cases) and using the same computer (Nvidia TITAN Xp 12 Gb GPU, Intel Xeon CPU E5-1620 v4 @ 3.50 GHz). The network was trained for 1000 epochs, using 1000 batches per epoch with a batch size of 500 spectra. We used Adam as our optimizer, set the base learning rate to be 0.005 and used an Euclidean loss function. The RF was trained on the entire dataset using 100 estimators and a maximum depth of 9. The distributions in Fig. 2a show that the absolute sO_2 estimation error of our proposed deep learning approach is considerably lower than the shallow RF network. The results (cf. Table 1) demostrate that our deep learning method can process up to 5.2×10^6 spectra per second with a median absolute sO_2 estimation error of 5.8% while the shallow RF regressor described in [13] processes spectra at a speed of 2.7×10^6 spectra per second with a median absolute sO_2 estimation error of 9.1% (cf. Table 1).

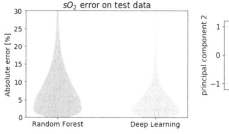 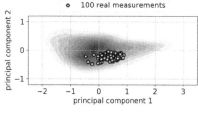

(a) Absolute sO_2 estimation error   (b) Principal component analysis

Fig. 2. (a) Absolute sO_2 estimation error distribution of our method (orange) compared to the RF reference method (blue). Values are capped at 30%. (b) *In vivo* brain MSI data (100 samples, randomly chosen) projected onto the first two principal components of the simulated data. (Color figure online)

Table 1. Performance of different parameter estimation methods on the *in silico* test data set. Given are the median absolute estimation error for sO_2, the interquartile range, as well as the regression speed in single spectrum inversions per second.

Method	$e_{\mathrm{abs}}^{sO_2}[\%]$	$e_{\mathrm{abs}}^{sO_2}[\%]$ IQR	Speed $[\frac{\mathrm{inv}}{s}]$
Reference method	9.1	(3.1, 11.8)	2.7×10^6
Our method	**5.8**	**(1.8, 6.7)**	$\mathbf{5.2 \times 10^6}$

3.2 *In Vivo* Qualitative Validation

To investigate whether our method is capable of detecting haemodynamic changes, we chose the monitoring of spreading depolarization (SD) in porcine brains as our target application. SD is a phenomenon in the brain related to the abrupt depolarization of neurons in gray matter which propagates in form of a wave [4]. It is well known to be coupled to haemodynamic responses with hypoxic components [12], making it a prime target for the qualitative validation of our method for functional MSI.

Induction of SDs. All experiments were performed in accordance with the relevant guidelines and regulations. Protocols for all experiments were approved by the institutional animal care and use committee in Karlsruhe, Baden-Wurttemberg, Germany (Protocol No. 35-9185.81/G-174/16). The procedure for inducing and measuring SDs was as follows: As shown in Fig. 3a, a craniotomy exposed the parietal cortex, and spreading depolarizations were induced using 2–5 µL Potassium Chloride (KCl) drops placed with a hamilton syringe in regions selected by visual inspection in the parietal cortex [8,9].

MSI Data Acquisition and Processing. For the MSI recordings, we applied the hardware described in Sect. 2.1. Our network was trained with the simulated data described in Sect. 2.2. As our camera performs sequential measurements, tissue motion caused by respiration, heart beat or surgical manipulation, for example, potentially lead to misalignments between the recorded images. This is an effect currently not explicitly simulated in the training data. In order to tackle this problem, we performed elastic registration as preprocessing step to the recorded data: To compensate for intra-frame motion, the images corresponding to individual bands of a whole MSI image were registered with the algorithm bUnwarpJ [3] incorporated in the software FIJI [7], which is based on elastic deformations. The band with highest contrast (560 nm) was used as reference.

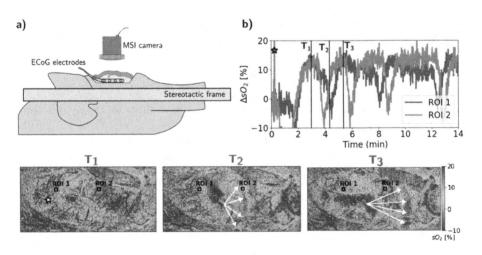

Fig. 3. SDs induced by KCl stimulation in the left hemisphere of a porcine brain. Here (a) shows the setup for monitoring spreading depolarizations with an MSI camera. Adapted from [5] published under creative commons. (b) shows time evolution of mean estimated tissue oxygenation %$sO2$ in two ROIs. The KCl injection time is indicated by a star. (c) shows estimated tissue oxygenation (%$sO2$) for the three time points (T1)–(T3). An animated video of the data can be found in the supplementary material of this paper.

Registration with this method of one complete MSI image takes 12 s. The implementation of such an elastic transformation to compensate brain movement was inspired by recent work of Scholl et al. [11]. It should be noted that such registration was implemented only with the purpose of obtaining a better visualization of haemodynamic changes; it is not a requirement of our proposed network model and intra-frame motion compensation is not necessary when applying a snapshot camera for image acquisition.

Results. According to a principal component analysis (PCA) similar to that performed in [15], the *in vivo* spectra recorded resemble the training data that we simulate (cf. Fig. 2b). Note that the first two components accounted for 96% of the variance of the training data. As demonstrated in Fig. 3, our method is capable of real-time visualization of blood oxygenation in the porcine cortex: After induction of KCl, SDs can be clearly visualized, as illustrated by the mean value of two regions of interest (ROIs) (cf. Fig. 3b).

4   Discussion

In this work, we presented a new approach to oxygenation estimation based on MSI and successfully applied it to visualize the phenomenon of SD in the gyrencephalic brain.

In the conducted *in silico* analysis, the RF performed worse than the proposed neural network both in terms of accuracy and speed. While the RF has to make a trade off between inference speed and accuracy, neural networks can be highly parallelized and run entirely on the GPU. However, it should be noted that the time needed to train a RF is significantly lower than for neural networks. It is worth mentioning that for big training data sets, a deeper RF might have to be trained, lowering the speed to significantly lower values. For instance, on our data set it was 3.6×10^5 spectra per second when using a maximum depth of 500 compared to 2.7×10^6 spectra per second when using a depth of 9.

In conclusion, the proposed method achieves high spatio-temporal resolution, outperforms state-of-the-art methods and can be adapted to any hardware setup. This makes it a potential powerful tool to examine haemodynamics not only in animals but also in humans.

References

1. Adler, T.J., et al.: Uncertainty-aware performance assessment of optical imaging modalities with invertible neural networks. Int. J. Comput. Assist. Radiol. Surg. **14**, 997–1007 (2019)
2. Alerstam, E., Lo, W., David, T.D., Rose, J., Andersson-Engels, S., Lilge, L.: Next-generation acceleration and code optimization for light transport in turbid media using GPUs. Biomed. Opt. Express **1**, 658–675 (2010)
3. Arganda-Carreras, I., Sorzano, C.O.S., Marabini, R., Carazo, J.M., Ortiz-de-Solorzano, C., Kybic, J.: Consistent and elastic registration of histological sections using vector-spline regularization. In: Beichel, R.R., Sonka, M. (eds.) CVAMIA

2006. LNCS, vol. 4241, pp. 85–95. Springer, Heidelberg (2006). https://doi.org/10.1007/11889762_8

4. Dreier, J.P., Reiffurth, C.: The stroke-migraine depolarization continuum. Neuron **86**, 902–922 (2015)

5. Kirchner, T., et al.: Photoacoustics can image spreading depolarization deep in gyrencephalic brain. Sci. Rep. **9**, 8661 (2019)

6. Moccia, S., et al.: Uncertainty-aware organ classification for surgical data science applications in laparoscopy. IEEE Trans. Biomed. Eng. **65**, 2649–2659 (2018)

7. Rueden, C.T., et al.: Image J2: ImageJ for the next generation of scientific image data. BMC Bioinform. **18**, 529 (2017)

8. Santos, E., et al.: Cortical spreading depression dynamics can be studied using intrinsic optical signal imaging in gyrencephalic animal cortex. In: Katayama, Y., Maeda, T., Kuroiwa, T. (eds.) Brain Edema XV. NEUROCHIRURGICA, vol. 118. Springer, Vienna (2013). https://doi.org/10.1007/978-3-7091-1434-6_16

9. Santos, E., et al.: Radial, spiral and reverberating waves of spreading depolarization occur in the gyrencephalic brain. NeuroImage **99**, 244–255 (2014)

10. Sassaroli, A., Fantini, S.: Comment on the modified Beer-Lambert law for scattering media. Phys. Med. Biol. **49**, N255–N257 (2004)

11. Schöll, M.J., Santos, E., et al.: Large field-of-view movement-compensated intrinsic optical signal imaging for the characterization of the haemodynamic response to spreading depolarizations in large gyrencephalic brains. J. Cereb. Blood Flow Metab. **37**, 1706–1719 (2017)

12. Takano, T., et al.: Cortical spreading depression causes and coincides with tissue hypoxia. Nat. Neurosci. **10**, 754–762 (2007)

13. Wirkert, S.J., et al.: Endoscopic sheffield index for unsupervised *In Vivo* spectral band selection. In: Luo, X., Reichl, T., Mirota, D., Soper, T. (eds.) CARE 2014. LNCS, vol. 8899, pp. 110–120. Springer, Cham (2014). https://doi.org/10.1007/978-3-319-13410-9_11

14. Wirkert, S.J., et al.: Robust near real-time estimation of physiological parameters from megapixel multispectral images with inverse Monte Carlo and random forest regression. Int. J. Comput. Assist. Radiol. Surg. **11**, 909–917 (2016)

15. Wirkert, S.J., et al.: Physiological parameter estimation from multispectral images unleashed. In: Descoteaux, M., Maier-Hein, L., Franz, A., Jannin, P., Collins, D.L., Duchesne, S. (eds.) MICCAI 2017. LNCS, vol. 10435, pp. 134–141. Springer, Cham (2017). https://doi.org/10.1007/978-3-319-66179-7_16

Open Access This chapter is licensed under the terms of the Creative Commons Attribution 4.0 International License (http://creativecommons.org/licenses/by/4.0/), which permits use, sharing, adaptation, distribution and reproduction in any medium or format, as long as you give appropriate credit to the original author(s) and the source, provide a link to the Creative Commons license and indicate if changes were made.

The images or other third party material in this chapter are included in the chapter's Creative Commons license, unless indicated otherwise in a credit line to the material. If material is not included in the chapter's Creative Commons license and your intended use is not permitted by statutory regulation or exceeds the permitted use, you will need to obtain permission directly from the copyright holder.

Towards a Cyber-Physical Systems Based Operating Room of the Future

Chin-Boon Chng, Pooi-Mun Wong, Nicholas Ho$^{(\boxtimes)}$, Xiaoyu Tan, and Chee-Kong Chui

Department of Mechanical Engineering,
National University of Singapore, Singapore, Singapore
nicholasho.jh@u.nus.edu

Abstract. Modern operating rooms require medical specialists to handle complex surgeries so that effective and yet safe treatment can be delivered. The development of a medical cyber-physical system is a highly multidisciplinary and challenging endeavour. In this paper, an intelligent surgical theatre (aka surgical theatre of the future) architecture was proposed based on Cyber-Physical System (CPS) concepts. The proposed architecture, which comprises of intelligence components, cyber components, cyber-physical interfaces and physical components, is specially designed to facilitate effective data/information exchanges among these components. The proposed architecture also accounts for three various stages of a typical surgical operation (i.e. pre-operation, intra-operation and post operation), which are all essential for the development of a complete CPS-based Operating Room of the Future (ORF). As higher levels of teamwork, communication and coordination can now be achieved with a system based on the proposed architecture, it has the potential to enhance safety, increase efficiency and reduce costs in the ORF.

Keywords: Operating theater · Cyberphysical systems · Management

1 Introduction

The operating room (OR) of today requires medical specialists to handle complex surgeries so that effective and yet safe treatment can be delivered. Hence, it is a high-risk, dynamic and stressful environment [1]. Despite attempts to reduce these negative factors by introducing advanced technologies and more specialists in the OR, the current ORs remain overcrowded and inefficient. For instance, the scans and data of patients are currently not well integrated or presented within a reasonable time frame in the OR. These inefficiencies can lead to a potential negative impact on the safety of the patient and costs [6]. According to statistics,

This work was supported in part by Singapore MOE FRC Tier 1 Grant (R265000-614-114). We wish to acknowledge the collaboration with the research group led by P.A. Heng of the Chinese University of Hong Kong on the development of the prototype robotic assisted ablation system.

© Springer Nature Switzerland AG 2019
L. Zhou et al. (Eds.): OR 2.0 2019/MLCN 2019, LNCS 11796, pp. 47–55, 2019.
https://doi.org/10.1007/978-3-030-32695-1_6

around 40% of surgery-related errors occur in the operating room. Because of increasing importance of safety, quality and efficiency in the healthcare industry, there is a need to gear towards the Operating Room of the Future (ORF) [1].

It is crucial to promote better integration of advanced technologies, and to improve teamwork, communication and coordination within the ORF [6]. It is also crucial to consider an information-based architecture that facilitates dataflow when developing the ORF; this promotes a more systematic approach for surgical procedures [1]. One solution to develop an ORF that will fulfil the stated requirements is to adopt Cyber-Physical System (CPS) technologies. CPSs generally involve an optimal mix of enabling advanced technologies with an aim to facilitate dataflow among physical and cyber components, and this leads to higher levels of communication and coordination within the OR [9,12,14]. For instance, collaboration between the physical and cyber components can be leveraged and the quality of process can be further improved with the introduction of intelligence components within the CPS [2]. Such systems that involve surgical processes have been an ongoing area of development and have been labeled as Medical CPS (MCPS) in the literature [7].

The development of a MCPS is a highly multidisciplinary and challenging endeavour with abundant literature describing implementations for a wide range of medical applications. Haque et al. [4] reviewed and categorized a multitude of such systems based on eight different elements. Six challenges for MCPS have been identified by Lee et al. [7]: high assurance software, interoperability, context awareness, autonomy, security and privacy, and certifiability. A number of recent works attempt to answer these challenges - Okamoto et al. [11] described the use of industrial middleware Open Robot/Resource interface for the Network (ORiN) proposed by the Japan Robot Association for the integration of medical devices in an operating room. Their work illustrated that the proposed MCPS can not only be constructed flexibly, but also effectively aids in the device exchange procedures. Similarly, Joerger et al. [5] has reported a successful proof of concept MCPS for management of a large suite of ORs at Houston Methodist Hospital. Their work illustrated the usefulness of the proposed MCPS to promote better communication, implementation efficiency and teamwork. Lastly, in the work of Li et al. [8], a MCPS was proposed specifically for the handling and monitoring of surgical instruments in the OR. It was concluded that the amount of human errors made in the OR can be eliminated when their MCPS was proposed, as the human involvement in these tasks is significantly reduced. Their proposed MCPS can potentially result in a safer and more accurate surgery process. Overall, these works illustrated the usefulness of MCPS to improve teamwork, efficiency, flexibility, communication and coordination during surgical procedures.

2   Methods

2.1   Intelligent Surgical Theatre Architecture

The future surgical theatre will compose of intelligence components, cyber components, cyber-physical interfaces and physical components (Fig. 1). There are four types of data/information exchange among the components. Reports are compiled and organized data as summaries to be interpreted by the sink. Analysis are processed data which information could provide insights to the sink to solve problems. Raw data are unprocessed data from the physical environment. Lastly, controls are input to cause corresponding responses in a control system.

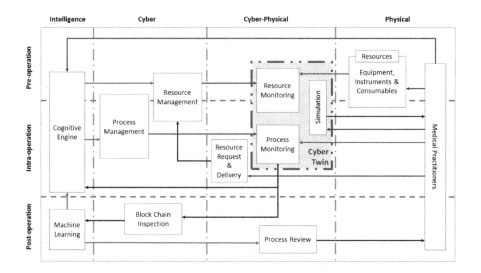

Fig. 1. Architecture of a operating room of the future

Each operation workflow could be sectioned into pre-operation, intra-operation and post operation. In pre-operation, assuming a pre-operation plan has been defined, organization and requisition of the required equipment, entry and preparation of patient based on the surgical plan is performed. The moment a medical practitioner lay a medical resource onto the patient, for example, the action of anesthetizing the patient, the surgery enters the intra-operation phase. Here, the surgical plan is executed, with surgeons adapting to complications based on SOPs and experience. Immediately after the surgical site of the patient is closed and the patient has stabilized enough to exit the operating theatre, the surgery enters the post-operation phase. In the post-operation phase, the process flow is reviewed and equipment is marked for sterilization and/or dispensed for other operations.

2.2 Cyber-Twin

The cyber components also include resource management and process management. The management systems utilizes analysis from the cognitive engine and
the information of available options to select resource and procedure to be taken
during the pre-operation and intra-operation phases. These management systems function mainly based on simple logics to make decisions. They are used
to control the actions of the monitoring system.

During the pre-operation phase, analysis from the cognitive engine suggests the list of surgical instruments required. The resource management system
commands the monitoring system at the entrance of the operation theatre to
itinerary check on instruments that were brought into the operation theatre. At
the same time, the resource management system also commands the monitoring system in the operation theatre to check the set-up of equipment that are
already in the room. On the other hand, based on the inputs from the cognitive
engine, the process management system will attempt to recommend a list of
suitable tasks that is specific to the given application; the medical practitioner
can choose to utilize the recommended process or customize his own process
based on his expertise and experience.

During the intra-operative phase, if an emergency has occurred and there
is a need of a new resource that is not in the operation theatre, the medical
practitioner could request for it from inside the room. The resource management
will notify the resource monitoring system to look out for the delivery status of
that resource until it arrives. On the other hand, the process management system
controls the process monitoring system to identify the current operation status.
The process monitoring system can be made up of various sensory systems to
collect relevant data, which will be sent to the intelligence system for sense-
making. Moreover, the process management system is able to better execute the
task monitoring process over time, due to the learning and analytical capabilities
of the supporting intelligence system (made up of cognitive engine, machine
learning and blockchain components).

The cyber-physical interface forms a communication bridge between the
cyber programs and the physical environment. During the intra-operative phase,
the medical practitioners interacts with the cyber components using this interface. Typically a user interface panel can be located in the operation theatre to
enable the medical practitioner to request for resources. To avoid the repeated
need for disinfection of such physical interfaces, alternate methodologies like
gesture based methods can be utilized to reduce the risk of contamination [15].
For added security, the use of biometric recognition in [10] can be integrated to
improve gesture-based interfaces by automatically identifying the operators who
are wearing gloves. The resource request and delivery system are connected to
the resource storage outside of operation theatre. The request will be managed
in a central system to allocate available resources. From the other end, any available staff could deliver the resource and send it into the theatre via a delivery
tunnel that automatically logs reports to the resource management and sterilizes
the resource.

The resource monitoring system compiles the resource data and sends them to the process monitoring system which mainly consists of cameras that tracks the on-going surgery procedure. During the pre-operation phase, the medical practitioner could set-up a simulation of the discussed procedure to confirm their decisions. The monitoring systems provide real-time update to the simulation on the resource available and the past processes that had happened. Simulation could also be played during the intra-operation phase if desired either via augmented reality or on monitor screen. Although the system is capable of making its own intelligent decisions, a field expert is still required to make the final decision as a precaution to system inaccuracy and/or error. The system is specially designed to recommend decision options, rather than to decide on behalf of the medical practitioner.

2.3   Cognitive Engine and Machine Learning

The intelligence components are made up of a cognitive engine that plays the role of inferencing and monitoring the resources and processes involved for the surgical operation. For context awareness, semantic approaches for cognitive engines have been explored for improving intelligence CPS. The key motivation is to enable the CPS to infer and adapt to new information or uncertainty, catching errors and mitigating risks before they occur. Typically, these methods utilize an expert knowledge base through the design of an ontology accessible by both humans and computers. During the pre-operation phase, the ontology is first designed by the medical practitioners as part of the planning process of the surgery. The cognitive engine will infer the resources required for the surgery as part of the checking process with the medical practitioner's decision. Detailed implementation of such a cognitive engine is described in [13]. Inference results from the cognitive engine will be sent to the resource and process management which stores the planned sequence and information of the matching resources to be used. The release of analysis to the management system depends on the reported context from the monitoring system. The analysis may also suggest alternatives to the medical practitioners based on the updated context. This augmented decision cross-checks with the surgeons' situational awareness via the cyber-physical interface, in case the surgeon misses some information due to information overload. After the operation, the knowledge can be directly updated by the results from the machine learning unit to improve on the planned surgery; this is only applicable for straightforward knowledge types. However, if the knowledge type(s) is too complicated and require significant additional problem solving, it is necessary for the medical practitioners to get involved in the knowledge updating process; they could utilize the results from the machine learning unit to aid them in this process.

During the post-operation phase, the machine learning unit ingests data from report generated by the block chain system that is part of the cyber component. The block chain system records the whole surgical processes and provides inspection logic on the quality of the operation. For example, the block chain could calculate the failing rate of performing a cut by a specific surgeon. The process can be reviewed on demand, meaning that the results could only be accessed if the authorized individual gives permission. Since the information stored in block chain is posted and mined with unique encryption, this provides added security to the patient and the medical practitioners' private and confidential records. The block chain component can also be further utilized to perform peer-to-peer validation of the surgical procedure. This will help enhance the process management system. By feeding the block chains into the machine learning unit, the system could provide adapted suggestions to the medical practitioners on the next operation on resource distribution and surgical procedure which can potentially lead to higher success rate.

3   RadioFrequency Ablation Needle Insertion Robot

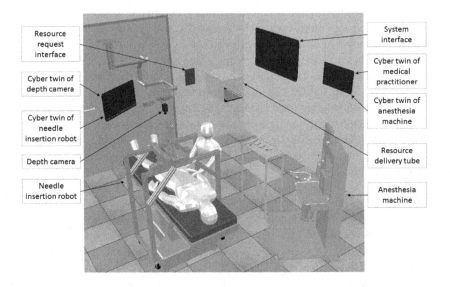

Fig. 2. Simulated layout of a RFA ablation system

In this section, the application of our proposed architecture for Radiofrequency Ablation (RFA) of liver tumors is described. The main aim of this case study is to illustrate the potential feasibility of the proposed architecture for surgical procedures. Hence, the chosen equipment and methods as mentioned in this case study example are meant for illustration purposes.

For this case study, a cognitive engine for the surgical process [13] and a robotic system for minimally invasive percutaneous RFA ablation [3] are adopted and integrated together with medical image processing, surgery pre-planning and Kinect-based vision registration to enable large and multiple RFA needle insertions to be performed with high accuracy, consistency and efficiency.

Figure 2 depicts a simulation of the OR with the resources required for the surgery. The constructed virtual, intelligent surgical theatre's physical components include various depth cameras, display monitors, resource delivery tubes, anaesthetic machine, and the needle insertion robot. Its cyber components, which are not visible in the figure itself, include the resource and process management systems and the blockchain inspection system. Interfacing between the physical and cyber components are its cyber-physical components, which include the cyber-twin modules for each of the physical components (e.g. patient, medical practitioners), resource request interface, and system interface.

Figure 3 depicts the data flow within the MCPS architecture. The needle insertion system utilizes an AR application, which is monitored by the Human Cyber-Twin, to dispense instructions to the human operator. The RFA system also involves a deep reinforcement learning algorithm, where data is retrieved by the Robot Cyber-Twin. The optimal policy from the learning algorithm will then determine the actions of the surgical robots based on the received data. Next, the RFA system involves calibration algorithms that are dependent on information (i.e. 3D imagery data of depth and colour measurements) received from the depth cameras. These calibration algorithms will process the data and send the results to the intelligence component via the Depth Camera Cyber-Twin and Blockchain System sub-components for phase recognition analysis and other forms of data analysis. Lastly, the role of the cloud is to facilitate data flow among the various components.

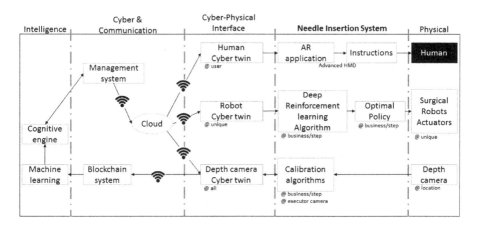

Fig. 3. Dataflow of the RFA ablation system within the MCPS architecture

4   Discussion and Conclusion

In this paper, an intelligent surgical theatre architecture was proposed based on CPS concepts. As higher levels of teamwork, communication and coordination can be potentially achieved with a system based on the proposed architecture, it has the potential to enhance safety, increase efficiency and reduce costs in the ORF. Moreover, the proposed system has the potential to overcome the various challenges (i.e. high assurance software, interoperability, autonomy, context awareness intelligence, device certifiability, security and privacy), which are mentioned by Lee et al. [7], in designing successful MCPS.

The RFA case study illustrates the potential of the proposed system to improve accuracy, consistency and efficiency for surgical processes, even when large and multiple surgical procedures are performed. As surgeries are generally complex procedures, the introduction of CPS utilizing intelligent subsystem and cyber-twins could help in the decision-making processes and facilitate effective and efficient data flow. However, the challenges, that may be faced in developing a successful CPS based on the proposed architecture, include requiring (a) to manage and maintain many subsystems at the same time, (b) heavy computing capabilities because of its intelligence and cyber-twin components, and (c) the involvement of the medical practitioner during the various operation phases.

For future works, we will first consult experienced surgeons to verify the challenges that are commonly faced in the OR and to verify the feasibility of the proposed architecture. To further develop our existing architecture, we will consider developing a model with an ontology that represents time explicitly for surgical processes. We will also conduct preliminary investigation of the proposed architecture via computer simulations to prove its feasibility. Future works will primarily include the physical development of the intelligent surgical theatre based on the proposed architecture. Experiments will be conducted based on a case study example to evaluate the developed system as a whole.

References

1. Bharathan, R., Aggarwal, R., Darzi, A.: Operating room of the future. Best Pract. Res. Clin. Obstet. Gynaecol. **27**(3), 311–322 (2013)
2. Delicato, F.C., Al-Anbuky, A., Wang, K.I.K.: Editorial: smart cyber-physical systems: toward pervasive intelligence systems. Future Gener. Comput. Syst. (2019)
3. Duan, B., et al.: Image-guided robotic system for radiofrequency ablation of large liver tumor with single incision. In: 2015 12th International Conference on Ubiquitous Robots and Ambient Intelligence (URAI), pp. 284–289. IEEE (2015)
4. Haque, S.A., Aziz, S.M., Rahman, M.: Review of cyber-physical system in healthcare. Int. J. Distrib. Sens. Netw. **10**(4), 217415 (2014)
5. Joerger, G., et al.: A cyber-physical system to improve the management of a large suite of operating rooms. ACM Trans. Cyber-Phys. Syst. **2**(4), 34 (2018)
6. Kopelman, Y., et al.: Trends in evolving technologies in the operating room of the future. J. Soc. Laparoendosc. Surg. **17**(2), 171–360 (2013)
7. Lee, I., et al.: Challenges and research directions in medical cyber-physical systems. Proc. IEEE **100**(1), 75–90 (2011)
8. Li, Y.T., Jacob, M., Akingba, G., Wachs, J.P.: A cyber-physical management system for delivering and monitoring surgical instruments in the OR. Surg. Innov. **20**, 377–384 (2012)

9. Liu, X.F., Shahriar, M.R., Al Sunny, S.N., Leu, M.C., Hu, L.: Cyber-physical manufacturing cloud: architecture, virtualization, communication, and testbed. J. Manuf. Syst. **43**, 352–364 (2017)
10. Nguyen, B.P., Tay, W.L., Chui, C.K.: Robust biometric recognition from palm depth images for gloved hands. IEEE Trans. Hum.-Mach. Syst. **45**(6), 799–804 (2015)
11. Okamoto, J., Masamune, K., Iseki, H., Muragaki, Y.: Development concepts of a smart cyber operating theater (SCOT) using orin technology. Biomed. Eng./Biomedizinische Technik **63**(1), 31–37 (2018)
12. Sturm, L.D., Williams, C.B., Camelio, J.A., White, J., Parker, R.: Cyber-physical vulnerabilities in additive manufacturing systems: a case study attack on the.STL file with human subjects. J. Manuf. Syst. **44**, 154–164 (2017)
13. Tan, X., et al.: Cognitive engine for robot-assisted radio-frequency ablation system. Acta Polytechnica Hungarica **14**(1), 129–145 (2017)
14. Wang, L., Törngren, M., Onori, M.: Current status and advancement of cyber-physical systems in manufacturing. J. Manuf. Syst. **37**, 517–527 (2015)
15. Wen, R., Tay, W.L., Nguyen, B.P., Chng, C.B., Chui, C.K.: Hand gesture guided robot-assisted surgery based on a direct augmented reality interface. Comput. Methods Programs Biomed. **116**(2), 68–80 (2014)

Proceedings of the 2nd International Workshop on Machine Learning in Clinical Neuroimaging: Entering the Era of Big Data via Transfer Learning and Data Harmonization (MLCN 2019)

Deep Transfer Learning for Whole-Brain FMRI Analyses

Armin W. Thomas[1,2] (iD), Klaus-Robert Müller[1,3,4], and Wojciech Samek[5](✉)

[1] Technische Universität Berlin, 10587 Berlin, Germany
athms.research@gmail.com, klaus-robert.mueller@tu-berlin.de
[2] Max Planck School of Cognition, 04103 Leipzig, Germany
[3] Korea University, Seoul 136-713, South Korea
[4] Max Planck Institute for Informatics, 66123 Saarbrücken, Germany
[5] Fraunhofer Heinrich Hertz Institute, 10587 Berlin, Germany
wojciech.samek@hhi.fraunhofer.de

Abstract. The application of deep learning (DL) models to the decoding of cognitive states from whole-brain functional Magnetic Resonance Imaging (fMRI) data is often hindered by the small sample size and high dimensionality of these datasets. Especially, in clinical settings, where patient data are scarce. In this work, we demonstrate that transfer learning represents a solution to this problem. Particularly, we show that a DL model, which has been previously trained on a large openly available fMRI dataset of the Human Connectome Project, outperforms a model variant with the same architecture, but which is trained from scratch, when both are applied to the data of a new, unrelated fMRI task. The pre-trained DL model variant is able to correctly decode 67.51% of the cognitive states from a test dataset with 100 individuals, when fine-tuned on a dataset of the size of only three subjects.

Keywords: fMRI · Decoding · Deep learning · Transfer learning

1 Introduction

Over the recent years, deep learning (DL) methods have been shown to outperform more conventional machine learning techniques in a variety of decoding tasks (for a review, see [8]). The success of DL methods is often attributed to their ability to autonomously learn highly abstracted representations of the raw input data, through a hierarchical sequence of non-linear transforms.

While researchers have started exploring the application of DL methods to the analysis of functional Magnetic Resonance Imaging (fMRI) data (e.g., [12]), their application to whole-brain fMRI data is still limited (e.g., [5] and [6]). Mainly, due to the small sample sizes and high dimensionality of fMRI datasets (and a lack of interpretability of DL models [7]). Particularly, in clinical settings, where fMRI datasets often only contain 10–20 patients and several hundred fMRI

© Springer Nature Switzerland AG 2019
L. Zhou et al. (Eds.): OR 2.0 2019/MLCN 2019, LNCS 11796, pp. 59–67, 2019.
https://doi.org/10.1007/978-3-030-32695-1_7

samples (i.e., volumes) per patient. Yet, each fMRI volume can easily contain several hundred thousand dimensions (i.e., voxels). In such classification settings, in which the number of data dimensions far exceeds the number of data samples, DL methods, as well as traditional machine learning approaches, are prone to overfitting (for a review, see [10]).

This problem has been similarly encountered in other research domains (e.g., [11]). Here, researchers have discovered that the successful application of DL models to small datasets can strongly benefit from *transfer learning*. Transfer learning describes a process in which a model is trained on one dataset and subsequently applied to another [11]. Thereby, the knowledge about the first dataset, contained in the parameter estimates of the trained model, is utilized to benefit the application of the model to the second dataset. This procedure often drastically improves the classification performance of the model, while also reducing the amount of time and data required to train it.

In this work, we explore whether transfer learning is similarly beneficial for the application of DL models to the decoding of cognitive states (e.g., viewing the image of a face vs the image of a house) from fMRI data. In particular, we show that a DL model that has been trained on the data of six out of seven task-fMRI datasets of the Human Connectome Project database [1] performs better in decoding the cognitive states underlying a seventh, unrelated task, when compared to a model variant that is trained entirely from scratch on the data of this task. For this comparison, we utilize the DeepLight framework [13], which decodes a cognitive state from whole-brain fMRI data, by combining convolutional and recurrent DL elements (see Fig. 1 and Sect. 2.2).

2   Methods

2.1   Data

Experiment Tasks. We analyzed the fMRI data of 400 unrelated participants in the following seven experiment tasks (for further details, see Table 1 and [1]):

- **Working Memory (WM):** Participants are asked to decide whether a currently presented image (of body parts, faces, places or tools) is the same as a previously presented target image.
- **Gambling:** Participants are asked to guess whether the value of a card (with values between 1–9) is below or above 5. Participants win or loose if they guess correctly/incorrectly. Trials are neutral if the value of the card is 5.
- **Motor:** Participants are presented with visual cues asking them to tap their left or right fingers, squeeze their left or right toes, or move their tongue.
- **Language:** Participants either hear a brief fable (story trials) or an arithmetic problem (math trials) and are subsequently given a two-alternative forced choice question about the story / arithmetic problem.
- **Social:** Participants are presented with short video clips of objects that either interact in some way or move randomly. Subsequently, participants are asked to decide whether the objects interacted with one another, did not have an interaction, or if they are not sure.

- **Relational:** Participants are presented with different shapes, filled with different textures. In relational trials, participants see a pair of objects at the top of the screen and a pair at the bottom. They are then asked to decide whether the bottom pair differs along the same dimension (shape or texture) as the top pair. In match trials, participants see one object at the top and bottom and are asked to decide whether the objects match on a specified dimension.
- **Emotion:** Participants are asked to decide which of two faces presented on the bottom of the screen matches the face at the top of the screen. The faces have an either angry or fearful expression.

Table 1. Overview of the fMRI Data. For each experiment task, the decoding targets (i.e., cognitive states), the number of decoding targets, the duration of the fMRI data, and the fraction of the entire dataset that the task's data make up are presented.

Task	Decoding targets	Target count	Duration (s)(%)
WM	Body, face, place, tool	4	400 s (19.19%)
Gambling	Win, loss, neutral	3	224 s (10.75%)
Motor	Left/right finger, left/right toe, tongue	5	312 s (14.97%)
Language	Story, math	2	480 s (23.03%)
Social	Interaction, no interaction	2	200 s (9.6%)
Relational	Relational, matching	2	216 s (10.36%)
Emotion	Fear, neutral	2	252 s (12.1%)
Total		**20**	**2,084 s (100%)**

FMRI Data. All analyzed fMRI data were provided in a preprocessed format by the Human Connectome Project (HCP), WU Minn Consortium (Principal Investigators: David VanEssen and Kamil Ugurbil; 1U54MH091657) funded by the 16 NIH Institutes and Centers that support the NIH Blueprint for Neuroscience Research; and by the McDonnell Center for Systems Neuroscience at Washington University. Whole-brain EPI acquisitions were acquired with a 32 channel head coil on a modified 3T Siemens Skyra with $TR = 720\,\text{ms}$ and $TE = 33.1\,\text{ms}$ (for further details on fMRI acquisition, see [14]).

FMRI Data Preprocessing. The HCP preprocessing pipeline for fMRI data [2] includes the following steps: gradient unwarping, motion correction, fieldmap-based EPI distortion correction, brain-boundary based registration of EPI to structural T1-weighted scan, non-linear registration into MNI152 space, and grand-mean intensity normalization (for further details, see [14] and [2]). In

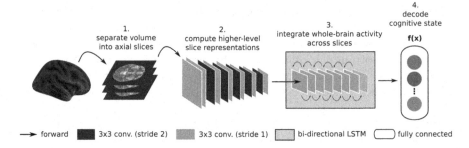

Fig. 1. Illustration of the DeepLight framework [13]. DeepLight first separates a whole-brain fMRI volume into a sequence of axial slices. Each axial slice is then processed by a convolutional feature extractor. The resulting sequence of higher-level axial slice representations is processed by a bi-directional LSTM unit, before a decoding prediction is made through a fully connected softmax output layer.

addition, we applied the following preprocessing: volume-based smoothing with a 3 mm Gaussian kernel, linear detrending and standardization of the single voxel signal time-series (resulting in a zero-centered voxel time-series with unit variance) and temporal filtering of the single voxel time-series with a butterworth highpass filter and a cutoff of 128 s. We further excluded the first two TRs of every fMRI experiment block (for experiment details, see [1]) from all analyses, as we did not expect any task-related hemodynamic response within this time period. Each fMRI volume contained $91 \times 109 \times 91$ voxels ($X \times Y \times Z$).

Data Splitting. We further divided the fMRI data into a distinct pre-training and test dataset, by assigning the data of the working memory task to the test data and all other experiment tasks to the pre-training data.

2.2   DeepLight

DeepLight [13] consists of three distinct computational modules (see Fig. 1). Namely, a feature extractor, an LSTM unit and output layer. To decode a cognitive state, DeepLight first separates a whole-brain fMRI volume into a sequence of axial slices. These slices are then sequentially processed by a convoltional feature extractor. The feature extractor used here consists of the following 12 convolution layers [9]: conv3-16(1), conv3-16(1), conv3-16(2), conv3-16(1), conv3-32(2), conv3-32(1), conv3-32(2). conv3-32(1), conv3-64(2), conv3-64(1), conv3-64(2), conv3-64(1) (notation: conv(kernel size) - (number of kernels)(stride size). All convolution kernels were activated through a rectified linear unit function. This sequence of convolution layers resulted in a 768-dimensional representation of each axial volume slice. To integrate the information provided by the resulting sequence of higher-level slice representations into a higher-level representation of the observed whole-brain activity, DeepLight applies a bi-directional LSTM

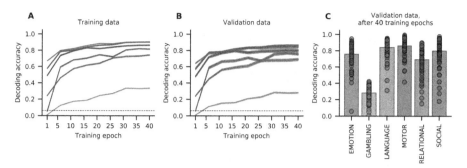

Fig. 2. DeepLight pre-training statistics. A-B: Mean decoding accuracy in the training (A) and validation (B) data, as a function of training epochs. C: Mean decoding accuracy in the validation data after 40 training epochs. Lines represent grand means, surrounded by standard error bands. Bar heights indicate grand means, while scatter points indicate subject means. Colors indicate tasks. Dashed lines indicate chance level. (Color figure online)

[4], containing two independent LSTM units. Each of the two LSTM units contains 64 neurons and iterates through the entire sequence of input slices, but in reverse order (one from bottom-to-top and the other from top-to-bottom). Lastly, to make a decoding decision, DeepLight applies a fully-connected softmax output layer, containing one output neuron per decoding target in the data.

Training. All DeepLight variants that were used in this study were trained as follows (if not reported otherwise): We iteratively trained DeepLight through backpropagation, by the use of the ADAM optimization algorithm, as implemented in tensorflow 1.13. During parameter estimation, we applied dropout regularization to all network layers as follows: We set the dropout probability to 50% for the LSTM unit and softmax output layer, For the convolution layers, however, we set the dropout probability to 0% for the first four convolution layers, 20% for the next four convolution layers, and 40% for the last four convolution layers (in line with [13]). We further used a learning rate of $1e^{-4}$ and a batch size of 24 fMRI volumes. DeepLight's weights were initialized by the use of a normal-distributed random initialization scheme [3].

3   Results

3.1   Pre-training Data

The goal of the first analysis was to pre-train DeepLight on the data of the six tasks contained in the pre-training dataset (see Sect. 2.1). To this end, we divided the data within each task into a distinct training and validation dataset, by assigning the data of 300 randomly selected subjects to the training data and the data of the remaining 100 subjects to the validation data. During pre-training, DeepLight's output layer contained 16 neurons, one for each cognitive

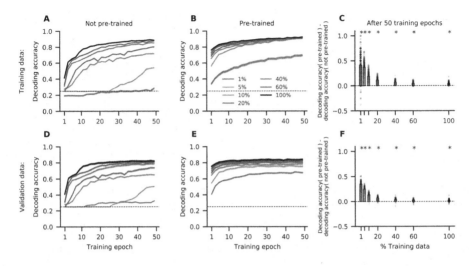

Fig. 3. Comparison of a "pre-trained" DeepLight variant with a "not pre-trained" variant that is trained entirely from scratch, when both are applied to subsets of 1%, 5%, 10%, 20%, 40%, 60%, and 100% of the full training dataset ($N = 300$) of the test task (the working memory task). A, B, D, E: Decoding accuracy as a function of training epochs in the training (A-B) and validation (D-E) data. C, F: Difference in decoding accuracy between the pre-trained and not pre-trained DeepLight variant after 50 training epochs. Stars indicate a statistically meaningful difference in a t-test using Bonferroni adjusted alpha levels of 0.05/7. Colors indicate the fraction of training data that is used. Lines show grand means with standard error bands surrounding them. Bar heights indicate grand means. Scatter points indicate subject means. (Color figure online)

state of each task in the pre-training dataset (for an overview, see Table 1). Thereby, DeepLight has no knowledge of the underlying tasks and is able to identify an individual's cognitive state without knowing which task the individual performed. Overall, we trained DeepLight for a period of 40 epochs (Fig. 2). Each epoch was defined as an iteration over the entire training data.

After 40 training epochs, DeepLight achieved an average decoding accuracy of 76.04% in the training dataset (Fig. 2A) and a decoding accuracy of 70.55% in the left-out validation data (Fig. 2B, C). DeepLight's average decoding accuracy was between 70.00–86.12% for five out of the six tasks in the validation data, while the decoding accuracy for the sixth task (the gambling task) was only 28.18%. When excluding the data of the gambling task from the decoding analysis, DeepLight's average decoding accuracy increased to 84.56% in the training dataset and 79.02% in the validation data.

3.2 Test Data

The goal of the second analysis was to explore the benefits of transfer learning for the application of DL models to fMRI data. To this end, we compared the performance of the pre-trained DeepLight variant (see Sect. 3.1) to that of a variant that was trained entirely from scratch, when both are applied to the data of the left-out test task (the working memory task, see Sect. 2.1). We again divided the data of the test task into a separate training and validation dataset, by randomly assigning 300 distinct subjects to the training data and the remaining 100 to the validation data. We then trained a DeepLight variant with transfer learning, and one without, on the training data of the test task. The output layer of both variants was set to contain four neurons (one per decoding target in the working memory task, see Table 1). Otherwise, the architecture and training procedures (see Sect. 2.2) of both variants were identical.

The first variant ("not pre-trained") does not apply transfer learning and was trained entirely from scratch, with weights initialized according to the normal-distributed random initialization scheme [3]. After 50 training epochs, this variant achieved an average decoding accuracy of 88.57% in the training data of the test task (Fig. 3A) and 81.91% in the validation data (Fig. 3D). The second variant ("pre-trained") applies transfer learning and is based on the DeepLight variant that we previously trained on the pre-training dataset (see Sects. 2.1 and 3.1). Particularly, we initialized the parameters of all network layers, except for the output layer (Fig. 1), to those weights obtained by the pre-trained DeepLight variant and only initialized the weights of the output layer according to the normal-distributed random initialization scheme [3]. After 50 training epochs, the pre-trained variant achieved an average decoding accuracy of 92.43% in the training data of the test task (Fig. 3B) and 83.83% in the validation data (Fig. 3E) and thereby performed meaningfully better in decoding the cognitive states from the validation data than the not pre-trained variant ($t(99) = 8.42, p < 0.0001$), Fig. 3F).

We were further interested in exploring how both DeepLight variants performed, when trained on smaller fractions of the original training dataset of the test task. Therefore, we repeatedly trained both variants on 1%, 5%, 10%, 20%, 40% and 60% of the full training dataset of the test task ($N = 300$), while evaluating their performance on the full validation data of the test task ($N = 100$). Overall, the pre-trained variant consistently achieved higher decoding accuracies in the training (Fig. 3C) and validation (Fig. 3F) data, and required less training time, when compared to the not pre-trained variant. Importantly, the pre-trained DeepLight variant already achieved an average decoding accuracy of 67.51% (Fig. 3E) in the validation data, when being trained on only 1% of the training dataset (equal to the data of three subjects). The not pre-trained variant, on the other hand, achieved a decoding accuracy of only 32.49% (Fig. 3D), when being trained on 1% of the training data and thereby performed meaningfully worse (the pre-trained DeepLight variant outperformed the not pre-trained variant by 35.02% ($t(99) = 49.68, p < 0.0001$)). Lastly, we also tested how much of the training data the pre-trained DeepLight variant requires to performs as well as (or better than) the not pre-trained variant that has been trained on the full training data. Interestingly, the pre-trained variant already achieved a meaningfully better decoding accuracy than the not pre-trained variant (which was trained on the full training dataset), when trained on only 40% of the training data ($t(99) = 2.82, p = 0.0057$).

4   Conclusion

The broad application of DL models to fMRI data is often hindered by the small sample size, and high dimensionality, of typical fMRI datasets. Here, we have demonstrated that transfer learning is beneficial for the application of DL models to small fMRI datasets. A DL model that has been pre-trained on a large, openly available fMRI dataset, generally requires less training data and time, and achieves higher decoding accuracies, when compared to a model variant with the same architecture that is trained entirely from scratch. The pre-trained model variant already performs well in decoding the cognitive states of 100 individuals in an unrelated fMRI task, when fine-tuned on a dataset of the size of only three subjects. However, future research is needed to explore how well the presented transfer learning approach generalizes to datasets outside of the Human Connectome Project [1].

References

1. Barch, D.M., Burgess, G.C., Harms, M.P., et al.: Function in the human connectome: task-fmri and individual differences in behavior. Neuroimage **80**, 169–189 (2013)
2. Glasser, M.F., Sotiropoulos, S.N., Wilson, J.A., et al.: The minimal preprocessing pipelines for the human connectome project. Neuroimage **80**, 105–124 (2013)
3. Glorot, X., Bengio, Y.: Understanding the difficulty of training deep feedforward neural networks. In: AISTATS, pp. 249–256 (2010)
4. Hochreiter, S., Schmidhuber, J.: Long short-term memory. Neural Comput. **9**(8), 1735–1780 (1997)
5. Huang, H., Hu, X., Zhao, Y., et al.: Modeling task fMRI data via deep convolutional autoencoder. IEEE Trans. Med. Imaging **37**(7), 1551–1561 (2017)
6. Jang, H., Plis, S.M., Calhoun, V.D., et al.: Task-specific feature extraction and classification of fmri volumes using a deep neural network initialized with a deep belief network: evaluation using sensorimotor tasks. NeuroImage **145**, 314–328 (2017)
7. Lapuschkin, S., Wäldchen, S., Binder, A., et al.: Unmasking clever hans predictors and assessing what machines really learn. Nature Commun. **10**, 1096 (2019)
8. LeCun, Y., Bengio, Y., Hinton, G.: Deep learning. Nature **521**(7553), 436 (2015)
9. LeCun, Y., Bengio, Y., et al.: Convolutional networks for images, speech, and time series. Handb. Brain Theory Neural Netw. **3361**(10), 1995 (1995)
10. Lemm, S., Blankertz, B., Dickhaus, T., Müller, K.R.: Introduction to machine learning for brain imaging. Neuroimage **56**(2), 387–399 (2011)
11. Oquab, M., Bottou, L., Laptev, I., Sivic, J.: Learning and transferring mid-level image representations using convolutional neural networks. In: Proceedings of the IEEE Conference on Computer Vision and Pattern Recognition, pp. 1717–1724 (2014)
12. Plis, S.M., Hjelm, D.R., Salakhutdinov, R., et al.: Deep learning for neuroimaging: a validation study. Front. Neurosci. **8**, 229 (2014)

13. Thomas, A.W., Heekeren, H.R., Müller, K.R., et al.: Analyzing neuroimaging data through recurrent deep learning models. arXiv preprint arXiv:1810.09945 (2018)
14. Uğurbil, K., Xu, J., Auerbach, E.J., et al.: Pushing spatial and temporal resolution for functional and diffusion mri in the human connectome project. Neuroimage **80**, 80–104 (2013)

Knowledge Distillation
for Semi-supervised Domain Adaptation

Mauricio Orbes-Arteainst[1,2,3,4(✉)], Jorge Cardoso[4], Lauge Sørensen[1,3],
Christian Igel[1], Sebastien Ourselin[4], Marc Modat[4], Mads Nielsen[1,3],
and Akshay Pai[2]

[1] Department of Computer Sceince, University of Copenhagen,
Copenhagen, Denmark
[2] Cerebriu A/S, Copenhagen, Denmark
[3] Biomediq A/S, Copenhagen, Denmark
[4] King's College London, London, UK
henry.m.orbes_arteaga@kcl.ac.uk

Abstract. In the absence of sufficient data variation (e.g., scanner and
protocol variability) in annotated data, deep neural networks (DNNs)
tend to overfit during training. As a result, their performance is significantly lower on data from unseen sources compared to the performance
on data from the same source as the training data. Semi-supervised
domain adaptation methods can alleviate this problem by tuning networks to new target domains without the need for annotated data from
these domains. Adversarial domain adaptation (ADA) methods are a
popular choice that aim to train networks in such a way that the features
generated are domain agnostic. However, these methods require careful
dataset-specific selection of hyperparameters such as the complexity of
the discriminator in order to achieve a reasonable performance. We propose to use knowledge distillation (KD) – an efficient way of transferring
knowledge between different DNNs – for semi-supervised domain adaption of DNNs. It does not require dataset-specific hyperparameter tuning, making it generally applicable. The proposed method is compared to
ADA for segmentation of white matter hyperintensities (WMH) in magnetic resonance imaging (MRI) scans generated by scanners that are not
a part of the training set. Compared with both the baseline DNN (trained
on source domain only and without any adaption to target domain) and
with using ADA for semi-supervised domain adaptation, the proposed
method achieves significantly higher WMH dice scores.

Keywords: Semi-supervised learning · Domain adaptation ·
Knowledge distillation · White matter hyperintensities

© Springer Nature Switzerland AG 2019
L. Zhou et al. (Eds.): OR 2.0 2019/MLCN 2019, LNCS 11796, pp. 68–76, 2019.
https://doi.org/10.1007/978-3-030-32695-1_8

1   Introduction

In the presence of a large training dataset that covers all possible data variations, deep neural networks (DNNs) can achieve super-human performance in image recognition and semantic segmentation tasks. However, in medical image segmentation tasks large annotated training datasets are often scarce. In addition, training and test data are drawn from different distributions. For example, the images were obtained using different scanners at different sites or the demographics of the subjects differ. This violation of the i.i.d. assumption (i.e., that training and test data are drawn independently from the same distribution) typically has the effect that the performance on the test data is significantly worse than on the training data.

Domain adaptation (DA) approaches try to alleviate the problem of applying models in new domains with different characteristics. In particular, semi-supervised DA methods provide a way to learn structure from unlabeled data in new domains. Among the several semi-supervised DA (SSL-DA) methods proposed, the most popular one is *adversarial training based domain adaptation* (ADA). ADA relies on generating features that are invariant with respect to a domain discriminator. ADA requires extensive parameter optimization due to the necessity of a robust discriminator. And a recent study pointed out the flaws in the evaluation of SSL-DA methods [1].

In this paper, we evaluate a modified *knowledge distillation* (KD) [2,3] method for generalizing DNNs to new domains with a common clinical problem in contrast to using ADA methods. The datasets chosen for evaluation not only involve different magnetic resonance images (MRIs), but also were acquired on subjects with different demographic makeup. Through our evaluation, we show that the proposed KD is generally able to achieve better dice scores in segmenting white matter hyperintensities (WMH) on datasets that are not a part of the training data and do not share any attributes when compared to baseline and ADA.

2   Related Work

Among the recent works on DA, several methods rely on using a small amount of data (*annotated*) to fine-tune a baseline model [4,5]. The performance of this approach not only relies on a new – albeit small – set of annotations but also on the choice of the set. In contrast, SSL-DA do not use data annotations on new target domains. Adversarial training is a popular SSL-DA method [6–8]. Here, networks are trained in such a way that the generated features are agnostic to the data domain with respect to a domain discriminator. A similar solution, ADA, was employed by [9] to adapt networks to be agnostic to domain changes.

Another class of DA method use KD to transfer representations between data domains. For instance, [10] proposed using KD to transfer knowledge between different modalities of the same scene. Closely related to our work is [11], where the authors propose to use omni-supervised learning (OSL) to include unlabelled data in the learning process. Here, data distillation is used to generate an ensemble of predictions from multiple transformations of unlabeled data, using a teacher model, to generate new training annotations. The proposed method differs from this method on two accounts: (a) Only soft labels are used to train the single student network, where the idea is to improve segmentation by learning label similarities from unannotated data (b) the data included in the training of the student involves data from new domains in small amounts in contrast to OSL.

3 Methods

In SSL-DA methods, we assume the source domain images and their annotations, $(x_s, y_s) \in \mathbf{X}_s$, are drawn from a distribution $p_s(x_s, y)$. The target domain images $x_t \in \mathbf{X}_t$, are drawn from a distribution $p_t(x_t, y)$ where there are no annotations available. We consider classification into K classes. In an ideal scenario, where p_s and p_t are sufficiently similar, the goal is to find a feature representation mapping f that maps an input to K scores, where the ith score models (up to a constant) the logarithm of the probability that the input belongs to class K. These scores can then be mapped by $\sigma : \mathbb{R}^K \to \mathbb{R}^K$ to probability maps over the classes. SSL-DA first finds a function f_s performing well on a source domain and then finds a new f_t based on f_s that performs well on the target domain. Vanilla supervised learning methods rely on including annotations from both $\mathbf{X}_s$ and $\mathbf{X}_t$.

In the popular ADA method, the goal is to minimize the distance between the empirical distributions of $p_s(f_s(\mathbf{X}_s)|y)$ and $p_t(f_t(\mathbf{X}_t)|y)$. Here, a discriminator D is a neural network that distinguishes between the two domains. Therefore, the discriminator acts as a discrepancy measure that brings the two distributions together. Overall, adversarial training involves train a network that generates f in a standard supervised manner that is indistinguishable by a discriminator [6,9].

3.1 Knowledge Distillation for Domain Adaptation

KD [2] was originally intended to compress neural networks with high number of parameters with networks of lower complexity. The objective is to teach a simpler student network to imitate a more complex trained teacher network, through a loss function called the distillation loss. To perform unsupervised domain adaptation, we proposed to use the teacher/student learning strategy. Specifically, the data from the source domain is used to train a teacher model in a supervised fashion. Then, the trained teacher is used to generate posterior probability maps or soft labels on the union of source and target data. These posterior probabilities are used instead of usual hard labels to train the student or target model. Note, this approach can take advantage of large amounts of unlabeled data acquired from any number of domains. An attractive feature of distillation loss is the soft representation of one-hot encoded label vectors which allow the student to be optimized over a smoother optimization landscape. Moreover, the smooth representation of labels also allows the learning of label similarities, which is particularly useful in learning boundaries in semantic segmentation tasks. The proposed semi-supervised learning method is formulated below.

Training the Teacher or Source Domain Model: Consider a set of N manually annotate images from a source domain $\mathbf{X}_s = \{(x_i, y_i), i = 1 \ldots N\}$, where $x_i \in \mathbb{R}^d$ represent a d-dimensional MR scan, with $v = 1 \ldots V$ voxels, and $y_i \in [0,1]^K$ with $\|y_i\|_1 = 1$ its correspondent label. Assuming there is a set F_s that holds functions $f : \mathbb{R}^d \to \mathbb{R}^K$ we aim to learn a feature representation f_s (teacher model) which follows the optimization of a loss function, l, according to Eq. (1)

$$\underset{f \in F_s}{\arg \min} \frac{1}{N} \sum_{x_i \in \mathbf{X}_s} l(y_i, \sigma(f_s(x_i))) \tag{1}$$

$$[\sigma(z)]_k = \frac{e^{[z]_k}}{\sum_{l=1}^{K} e^{[z]_l}} \tag{2}$$

In a standard supervised learning way, the teacher network is optimized using the cross-entropy loss function (or any differentiable loss function of choice).

Training the Student or Target Model: Even though f_s is suitable to segment the images from the source domain $\mathbf{X}_s$, it may not be suitable for data coming from a different data distribution $\mathbf{X}_t$. Our goal is find a function $f_t \in F_t$, which is suitable to segment data from $\mathbf{X}_t$. Assuming, we have access to a limited set of unlabeled scans in the target domain $\mathbf{X}_t = \{x_i, i = 1 \ldots M\}$, we can then create a set

$$\mathbf{X}_U = \{(x_i, y_i) \,|\, x_i \in \mathbf{X}_s, y_i = f_s(x_i), 1 \le i \le N\} \cup$$
$$\{(x_i, y_i) \,|\, x_i \in \mathbf{X}_t, y_i = f_s(x_i), 1 \le i \le M\}$$

that may be used to optimize a student using the distillation loss. Through soft-representations of this union dataset, the student is expected to learn a better mapping to the labels than the teacher network. When training the student network, we consider probability distributions over the labels as targets, not single classes. This representation reflects the uncertainty of the prediction by the teacher network. The function f_t is found by (approximately) solving,

$$\underset{f \in F_t}{\arg \min} \frac{1}{(N+M)} \sum_{x_i \in \mathbf{X}_U} l(\sigma(T^{-1}f_s(x_i)), \sigma(f_t(x_i))) \ , \tag{3}$$

Here, $T > 1$ is the temperature parameter which controls the softness of the class probability prediction given by f_s.

4 Experiments and Results

4.1 Databases

The **WMH segmentation challenge** (https://wmh.isi.uu.nl/) dataset is a public database that contains T1-weighted and FLAIR scans for 60 subjects from three different clinics. The data also consists of manual annotations of WMH from presumed vascular origin. T1-weighted images have been registered to FLAIR since annotations were performed in this space. The images were also corrected for bias field inhomogenities using SPM12. An important feature of this dataset is that the scanners and demographics have variance as show in the Table 1.

Table 1. Summary of data characteristics in the WMH challenge database

Clinic	Scanner name	Voxel size(m^3)	Size	# of images
Utrech	3T Philips Achieva	$0.96 \times 0.95 \times 3.00$	$240 \times 240 \times 48$	20
Singapore	3T Siemens TrioTim	$1.00 \times 1.00 \times 3.00$	$252 \times 232 \times 48$	20
Amsterdam	3T GE Signa HDxt	$1.20 \times 0.98 \times 3.00$	$132 \times 256 \times 83$	20

4.2 Experimental Setup

One of the main objectives of the paper is to use semi-supervised learning to perform domain adaptation. We use the WMH challenge dataset to perform cross-clinical experiments in segmenting WMH on FLAIR images. We consider several scenarios to establish the performances of ADA and KD. The scenarios are described below. Note that, to evaluate the performance of the algorithms, dice overlap measures are used throughout.

- Lower bound baseline, **L-bound**: Here a baseline DNN model is trained on the source dataset to establish a lower bound performance. The DNN is trained on the source domain images henceforth referred to as **S**, and tested on 20 subjects from a target dataset **T**.
- Upper bound baseline, **U-bound**: Here, a baseline DNN model is trained like L-Bound, however, the training dataset is a union of images from both **S** and a subset of **T** (10 subjects, with annotations). The network is evaluated on the remaining 10 subjects in **T**.
- Adversarial domain adaptation, **ADA**: Following [9], we attempt at training a DNN model that is invariant to data domains. In this paper, to be consistent with KD, we train the domain discriminator based on the final layer of the baseline, in contrast to what was proposed in [9]. We use a discriminator composed of 4 convolutional layers with 8, 16 32, 64 number of filters, followed by 3 fully connected layers with 64, 128 and 2 neurons. For this experiment, like U-bound, the training dataset is a union of images from both **S** and a subset of **T** (10 subjects, without annotations). The network is evaluated on the remaining 10 subjects in **T**.
- Knowledge distillation, **KD**: The experimental setup for KD is the same as ADA. A temperature of 2 is used in the softmax for the distillation loss. The student network trained is identical to the teacher network whose architecture is a standard UNet (like L-bound, U-bound, and ADA) optimized with an

ADAM loss function and a learning rate of 10^{-4} with is gradual decrease after epoch 150. The network is trained for 400 epochs.

- Adaptation on-the-fly: A clinically relevant scenario is adapting to a small set of test images on the fly by keeping the teacher/baseline model constant. To validate this scenario, we apply ADA and KD on the same 10 unannotated **T** that are included in the training, but subject-wise. In other words, separate adaptation is performed on each instance of **T**, instead of including them together.

4.3 Results

Various combinations of mismatched (in terms of clinics) training and testing data were used. For instance, if the training data is from clinic 1 (Utrecth), the testing data is from either clinic 2 (Singapore), or clinic3 (Amsterdam). We did not test on two different clinics even though this scenario is practical. Table 2 illustrates mean dice coefficients (two folds) for each of the scenarios mentioned in Sect. 4.2 except for adaptation on the fly which is illustrated in Table 3. KD outperformed ADA in nearly all scenarios except for domain adaptation from Singapore clinic to Utrecht clinic and vice versa. For domain adaptation from Utrecht clinic to Singapore clinic, ADA was significantly better than KD. In the vice-versa situation, KD achieved a better mean which is statistically not significant. In all other scenarios, KD yielded statistically better dice overlaps compared to ADA. Note that the statistical comparison are made only between

Table 2. Illustrates dice overlaps (with variance). Bold fond indicates statistical significance at 5%, p-values (paired-sample t-test at was used to computed p-values, which were $0.0002 < p < 0.02$). Only ADA and KD methods are considered in the statistical comparison.

Training	Test			
	Method	Utrech	Singapore	Amsterdam
Utrech	L-bound		0.6126 (0.1092)	0.7207 (0.0793)
	ADA		**0.7004 (0.1057)**	0.7144 (0.0968)
	KD		0.6456 (0.0905)	**0.7548 (0.0755)**
	U-bound		0.8031 (0.1148)	0.7704 (0.0787)
Singapore	L-bound	0.6693 (0.2271)		0.7368 (0.0931)
	ADA	0.6859 (0.2036)		0.7337 (0.0912)
	KD	0.6924 (0.2103)		**0.7499 (0.0877)**
	U-bound	0.7063 (0.2016)		0.7699 (0.0851)
Amsterdam	L-bound	0.6471 (0.2086)	0.6811 (0.1172)	
	ADA	0.6800 (0.2128)	0.7202 (0.1154)	
	KD	**0.6909 (0.2135)**	**0.7482 (0.0975)**	
	U-bound	0.7208 (0.1851)	0.7988 (0.0869)	

Table 3. Mean dice overlaps from the adaptation-on-the-fly scenario. Bold fond indicates statistical significance at 5%, p-values (paired-sample t-test at was used to computed p-values, which were $0.0003 < p < 0.04$). Only ADA and KD methods are considered in the statistical comparison.

Training	Test			
	Method	Utrech	Singapore	Amsterdam
Utrech	KD		**0.6285 (0.097**	**0.7465 (0.0855)**
	ADA		0.7075 (0.095)	0.7220 (0.0995)
Singapore	KD	**0.6945 (0.1825)**		0.7425 (0.0805)
	ADA	0.6680 (0.1945)		0.7370 (0.0880)
Amsterdam	KD	**0.6745 (0.2005)**	**0.7395 (0.1165)**	
	ADA	0.6625 (0.1890)	0.7100 (0.1125)	

ADA and KD. In the adaptation-on-the-fly scenario, KD yields significantly better dice overlaps on a majority of the scenarios, the superior performance of ADA remains in the experiment that involves domain adaptation from Utrecht clinic to Singapore clinic. However, in the vice-versa scenario, KD performance better than ADA. To illustrate the differences in segmentations between KD and ADA, we plot the segmentations (scenario, Utrecht clinic to Amsterdam clinic) in Fig. 1. As illustrated, both the methods perform quite well in segmenting lesions with relatively larger volume, however, the main difference is evident in segmenting smaller lesions, specially in the deep white matter regions. It is interesting to note that the adaptation-on-the-fly and the classical scenarios yield nearly the same dice indicating a good generalisability and less dependency on the choice of the small dataset coming from the target domain.

| Target | ADA | KD | U-bound |

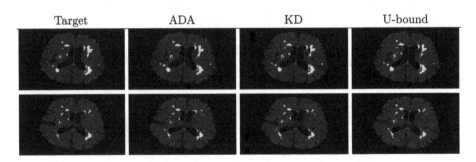

Fig. 1. Illustration of the segmentation's obtained with different methods trained on the Utrecht dataset and tested on the Amsterdam dataset. The top and bottom row illustrate segmentations on two different subjects.

5 Discussion

The main objective of this paper was to present domain adaptation from a semi-supervised learning perspective. We have evaluated a modified knowledge distillation approach and compared it to the popular adversarial approach under different clinical scenarios. Overall, the knowledge distillation approach gave better results and is relatively simpler to design when compared to the more architecture-dependent adversarial approaches. Adversarial approaches require extensive tuning of DNN architectures, especially for the discriminator, in order to achieve reasonable performances. In contrast, KD only involves choosing the temperature parameter which can be chosen only based on the performances on the source domain. One of the interesting outcomes is the inferior performance of KD on domain adaptation in scenario, Utrecht clinic to Singapore clinic. One of the reasons may be attributed to not just scanner differences but also differences in demographics. This may have led to an inferior teacher performance that the student network relies on. To verify this, we used the improved network from domain adaptation using ADA as a teacher and then trained a student based on it. We observed that the mean dice overlap improved from $0.65 \rightarrow 0.69$.

In future work, we will consider combining the adversarial approaches with knowledge distillation to improve the generalisability of DNNs across domains without the need for large annotated datasets.

Acknowledgements. This project has received funding from the EU H2020 under the Marie Skłodowska-Curie grant agreement No 721820.

References

1. Oliver, A., Odena, A., Raffel, C.A., Cubuk, E.D., Goodfellow, I.: Realistic evaluation of deep semi-supervised learning algorithms. In: Advances in Neural Information Processing Systems, pp. 3239–3250 (2018)
2. Hinton, G., Vinyals, O., Dean, J.: Distilling the knowledge in a neural network. arXiv preprint arXiv:1503.02531 (2015)
3. Lopez-Paz, D., Bottou, L., Schölkopf, B., Vapnik, V.: Unifying distillation and privileged information. arXiv preprint arXiv:1511.03643 (2015)
4. Hoffman, J., Rodner, E., Donahue, J., Darrell, T., Saenko, K.: Efficient learning of domain-invariant image representations. arXiv preprint arXiv:1301.3224 (2013)
5. Karani, N., Chaitanya, K., Baumgartner, C., Konukoglu, E.: A lifelong learning approach to brain MR segmentation across scanners and protocols. In: Frangi, A.F., Schnabel, J.A., Davatzikos, C., Alberola-López, C., Fichtinger, G. (eds.) MICCAI 2018. LNCS, vol. 11070, pp. 476–484. Springer, Cham (2018). https://doi.org/10.1007/978-3-030-00928-1_54
6. Tzeng, E., Hoffman, J., Saenko, K., Darrell, T.: Adversarial discriminative domain adaptation. In: Proceedings of the IEEE Conference on Computer Vision and Pattern Recognition, pp. 7167–7176 (2017)
7. Sun, B., Saenko, K.: Deep CORAL: correlation alignment for deep domain adaptation. In: Hua, G., Jégou, H. (eds.) ECCV 2016. LNCS, vol. 9915, pp. 443–450. Springer, Cham (2016). https://doi.org/10.1007/978-3-319-49409-8_35

8. Hoffman, J., et al.: Cycada: cycle-consistent adversarial domain adaptation. arXiv preprint arXiv:1711.03213 (2017)
9. Kamnitsas, K., et al.: Unsupervised domain adaptation in brain lesion segmentation with adversarial networks. In: Niethammer, M., et al. (eds.) IPMI 2017. LNCS, vol. 10265, pp. 597–609. Springer, Cham (2017). https://doi.org/10.1007/978-3-319-59050-9_47
10. Gupta, S., Hoffman, J., Malik, J.: Cross modal distillation for supervision transfer. In: Proceedings of the IEEE Conference on Computer Vision and Pattern Recognition, pp. 2827–2836 (2016)
11. Huang, R., Noble, J.A., Namburete, A.I.L.: Omni-supervised learning: scaling up to large unlabelled medical datasets. In: Frangi, A.F., Schnabel, J.A., Davatzikos, C., Alberola-López, C., Fichtinger, G. (eds.) MICCAI 2018. LNCS, vol. 11070, pp. 572–580. Springer, Cham (2018). https://doi.org/10.1007/978-3-030-00928-1_65

Relevance Vector Machines for Harmonization of MRI Brain Volumes Using Image Descriptors

Maria Ines Meyer[1,2](✉), Ezequiel de la Rosa[1], Koen Van Leemput[2,3], and Diana M. Sima[1]

[1] icometrix, Leuven, Belgium
{ines.meyer,ezequiel.delarosa,diana.sima}@icometrix.com
[2] Department of Health Technology, Technical University of Denmark, Lyngby, Denmark
[3] Martinos Center for Biomedical Imaging, Massachusetts General Hospital and Harvard Medical School, Boston, MA, USA
kvle@dtu.dk

Abstract. With the increased need for multi-center magnetic resonance imaging studies, problems arise related to differences in hardware and software between centers. Namely, current algorithms for brain volume quantification are unreliable for the longitudinal assessment of volume changes in this type of setting. Currently most methods attempt to decrease this issue by regressing the scanner- and/or center-effects from the original data. In this work, we explore a novel approach to harmonize brain volume measurements by using only image descriptors. First, we explore the relationships between volumes and image descriptors. Then, we train a Relevance Vector Machine (RVM) model over a large multi-site dataset of healthy subjects to perform volume harmonization. Finally, we validate the method over two different datasets: (i) a subset of unseen healthy controls; and (ii) a test-retest dataset of multiple sclerosis (MS) patients. The method decreases scanner and center variability while preserving measurements that did not require correction in MS patient data. We show that image descriptors can be used as input to a machine learning algorithm to improve the reliability of longitudinal volumetric studies.

Keywords: RVM · Harmonization · MRI · Brain volumes

1 Introduction

Large scale multi-site studies are of extreme importance in neuroimaging, both for research purposes and in clinical practice. Such studies face several challenges

This project received funding from the European Union's Horizon 2020 research and innovation program under the Marie Sklodowska-Curie grant agreement No 765148.

© Springer Nature Switzerland AG 2019
L. Zhou et al. (Eds.): OR 2.0 2019/MLCN 2019, LNCS 11796, pp. 77–85, 2019.
https://doi.org/10.1007/978-3-030-32695-1_9

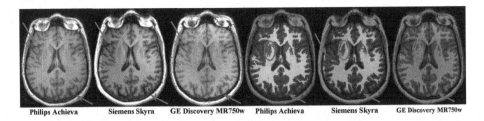

| Philips Achieva | Siemens Skyra | GE Discovery MR750w | Philips Achieva | Siemens Skyra | GE Discovery MR750w |

Fig. 1. MR images from same patient in different scanners. **Left side:** T1-weighted images. **Right side:** white matter segmentations obtained using the same method

due to hardware- or center-related variability. It is well known that scanner-factors such as manufacturer, magnetic field and gradient non-linearly influence volume measurements [4,14] obtained from structural Magnetic Resonance Imaging (MRI). At the image level, these factors are coupled with a high variability of intensities across patients and scanners, which can affect tasks like the segmentation of brain structures [16]. This effect is exemplified in Fig. 1, where three T1-weighted MR images from the same patient obtained on different scanners and their corresponding segmentations are represented.

The need to address multi-scanner and -center data harmonization is evidenced in the follow-up of Multiple Sclerosis (MS) patients. These patients exhibit an increased rate of brain atrophy when compared to healthy subjects, which has been linked to impairment [1]. However, it has been suggested that brain atrophy can only be reliably estimated over periods of at least five years [2], due to the variability caused by scanner and center factors.

Besides image processing approaches that aim at matching image intensity distributions to provide a more consistent input to the segmentation method [11,12], recent studies have focused on statistical harmonization of volumetric measurements based on scanner- or center-specific information. This type of methods generally apply regression techniques to correct measurements. Linear mixed-effects models using patient- and scanner-specific information as random effects were explored by [5] and [8]. Recently, [6] used an algorithm devised for genomics that extends the same type of model to account for site-specific factors. A data-driven approach based on independent component analysis was explored by [4], where correction was performed by selecting independent components related to scanning parameters. However, since these methods rely on scanner- or acquisition-specific information, they do not generalize and need to be adapted when used in new settings. Additionally, such information can be incomplete, especially in historical data. As such, it would be of interest to use information that is encoded in the images themselves, or that can be extracted from the volume quantification method to build more robust and adaptive techniques.

To address these issues, in this paper we present a novel statistical harmonization approach based on image descriptors and a machine learning algorithm. We first explore the relations between image-extracted properties and brain volume measurements that we could further exploit for harmonization. We then train a machine learning algorithm based on Automatic Relevance Determination on healthy data to perform volumetric corrections. We validate the method on a set of unseen healthy controls, and finally test it on a test-retest dataset of MS patients.

2   Data

Healthy Subjects. This dataset comprises 1996 T1-weighted (T1w) MRI scans from healthy subjects. The data is a compilation of several public datasets, such as [3, 10], and some proprietary data. The overall set comprises data from several different centers and scanner types from the major vendors (Siemens, Philips, GE). Magnetic field strengths (1.5T or 3T) and T1w sequence types also vary. For most of the data we have information regarding age and sex of the subject, scanner type, magnetic field strength and additional acquisition parameters like echo time (TE) and repetition time (TR). For building and testing our model, we randomly divided the data into training (70%) and test sets (30%).

Patient Data. To further validate the approach we test it in a dataset containing data from 10 MS patients as detailed in [7]. Each patient was scanned twice in three different 3 T scanners: *Philips Achieva, Siemens Skyra* and *GE Discovery MR450w.* An example is depicted in Fig. 1. We observed that one of the patients was an extreme case, showing very enlarged ventricles. Given that the volumetric measurements in such a case are prone to errors and are considered unreliable, this patient's data was discarded from further analysis.

2.1   Data Pre-processing and Feature Extraction

For each image we compute gray matter (GM) and white matter (WM) volumes using the well established atlas-based method described in [7]. Whole brain (WB) volume is then defined as the sum of WM and GM volumes.

We are interested in descriptors related to the T1w images that encode information about errors and bias in brain segmentations. Since the quality of a segmentation depends on a good registration to the atlas and is influenced by the contrast and noise present in an image, it is valuable to explore features that convey such information. We extract a total of 16 features of two main types: (i) Alignment information regarding the registration of the T1w image to the MNI atlas space, which includes decomposing the affine transformation (rotation angles, scale and shear factors in three directions), and measuring the similarity between the registered images using Normalized Mutual Information (NMI); and (ii) Contrast to Noise Ratio (CNR) between tissue types and between different brain structures (*e.g.*, lobes and cerebellum). CNR is given by:

$$CNR_{t_1,t_2} = \sqrt{2} \frac{|\bar{I}_{t_1} - \bar{I}_{t_2}|}{\sqrt{\sigma_{t_1}^2 + \sigma_{t_2}^2}},$$

where $\bar{I}_t$ represents the mean intensity of some tissue or structure t and σ_t^2 is the variance of the image intensities across this structure. We compute CNR_{t_1,t_2} by taking t_1 as the tissue or structure with higher average image intensity than t_2.

The brain volumes and some of the computed descriptors (*e.g.*, CNR and NMI) are known to be age dependent [13]. As such, age is used as a feature at training time, but not at test time. For analysis and comparison, we age-detrend the volumes by subtracting an age-matched estimated median value. CNR and NMI are corrected by fitting a linear regressor to the data.

3   The Relevance Vector Machine for Data Harmonization

To harmonize brain volumes, we subtract correction terms based on estimated variability trends from the original volumes. To determine the variation in the volumetric data that can be explained by the aforementioned image descriptors, we fit a linear model using the extracted features as independent variables. When choosing the model, we take a few important considerations into account: (i) we have 16 image-extracted features plus age; (ii) some of these are related only to one of the brain volumes; (iii) the features are not always unrelated; and (iv) we are interested in a probabilistic model, to capture uncertainty in our predictions. Given that standard generalized linear models do not address all these considerations, we investigate using a probabilistic machine learning technique.

The *Relevance Vector Machine* (RVM) is defined within a fully probabilistic framework and includes a mechanism of *automatic relevance determination* [9]. As described in [15], the model defines a conditional distribution for real-valued input-target vector pairs $\{\mathbf{x}_n, t_n\}_{n=1}^N$, of the type: $p(t_n|\mathbf{x}_n) = \mathcal{N}(t_n|y(\mathbf{x}_n), \beta^{-1})$, which specifies a Gaussian distribution over t_n with mean $y(\mathbf{x}_n)$ and precision (inverse variance) β. Here $\{\mathbf{x}_n\}_{n=1}^N$ are the set of extracted features and $\{t_n\}_{n=1}^N$ the corresponding volume measurement for each image n in a training dataset of size N. The function $y(\mathbf{x})$ is given by a linear combination of basis functions $\boldsymbol{\Phi}(\mathbf{x}) = (\Phi_1(\mathbf{x}), \ldots, \Phi_N(\mathbf{x}))$ with weights $\mathbf{w} = (w_0, \ldots, w_N)^{\mathrm{T}}$:

$$y(\mathbf{x}) = \sum_{i=1}^N w_i \Phi_i(\mathbf{x}) + w_0 = \boldsymbol{\Phi}(\mathbf{x})\mathbf{w},$$

where the ith basis function $\Phi_i(\mathbf{x}) \equiv K(\mathbf{x}, \mathbf{x_i})$ is a kernel centered around the ith training sample. In order to avoid over-fitting due to the large numbers of parameters in the model, a zero-mean Gaussian prior probability distribution is defined over the weights $\mathbf{w}$. Moreover, a separate hyperparameter α_i is introduced for each individual weight w_i, representing the precision of the corresponding weight:

$$p(\mathbf{w}|\boldsymbol{\alpha}) = \prod_{i=0}^N \mathcal{N}(w_i|0, \alpha_i^{-1}),$$

where $\boldsymbol{\alpha} = (\alpha_0, \ldots, \alpha_N)^{\mathrm{T}}$. Using the resulting model, relevance vector learning searches for the hyperparameters $\boldsymbol{\alpha}$ and β that maximize the marginal likelihood $p(\mathbf{t}|\boldsymbol{\alpha}, \beta)$ of the training data, where $\mathbf{t} = (t_1, \ldots, t_N)^{\mathrm{T}}$. Defining $\boldsymbol{\Phi}$ as the $N \times N$

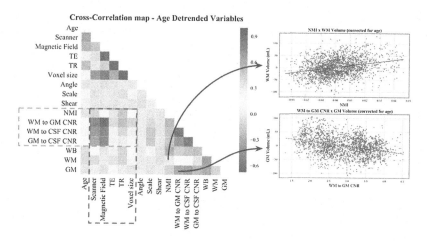

Fig. 2. Left: Cross-correlations between age-detrended brain volumes (mL) and extracted features. We represent *angle, shear* and *scale* as the result of multiplying the three directions. Right: a zoomed-in view of the relationship between volumes and image descriptors: top WM vs. NMI and bottom GM vs. CNR

matrix with $\boldsymbol{\Phi}(\mathbf{x}_n)$ in n^{th} row, the learning algorithm proceeds by iteratively updating $\boldsymbol{\alpha}$ and β as follows [15]:

$$\alpha_i^{new} = \frac{\gamma_i}{\mu_i^2} \quad \text{and} \quad (\beta^{new})^{-1} = \frac{\|\mathbf{t} - \boldsymbol{\Phi}\boldsymbol{\mu}\|^2}{N - \sum_i \gamma_i} \quad \text{with} \quad \gamma_i \equiv 1 - \alpha_i \Sigma_{ii},$$

where $\boldsymbol{\Sigma} = \left(\beta \boldsymbol{\Phi}^{\mathrm{T}} \boldsymbol{\Phi} + \mathrm{diag}(\boldsymbol{\alpha})\right)^{-1}$ and $\boldsymbol{\mu} = \beta \boldsymbol{\Sigma} \boldsymbol{\Phi}^{\mathrm{T}} \mathbf{t}$ are the posterior covariance and mean for the weights, respectively. In practice, during re-estimation, many α_i's tend to infinity, which causes the posterior distributions of the corresponding weights to peak around zero. The basis functions associated with these do not influence the predictions and can be pruned out, resulting in a sparse model. The remaining training samples with non-zero weights are called *relevance* vectors.

Once the model is trained, we can take a set of descriptors $\mathbf{x}_*$ of an unseen image, and try to predict the corresponding volume based on these descriptors alone using the posterior mean $\boldsymbol{\mu}$: $y_* = \phi(\mathbf{x}_*)\boldsymbol{\mu}$. Finally, we can obtain a *corrected* volume y_{corr} by subtracting the estimated contribution of the image descriptors from the original volume y: $y_{corr} = y - \phi(\mathbf{x}_*)\boldsymbol{\mu}$.

4 Results

4.1 Verification of Observable Correlations in Data

To verify whether there are correlations between image descriptors and the measured volumes, we built a cross-correlation map between these variables (see

Table 1. Median and standard deviation of age-detrended volumes (mL) before and after applying the RVM-based correction with different kernels (linear and RBF). Data pertains to the scanner-wise distribution of the test set (as in Fig. 3).

	WM		GM			WB	
Kernel	Median	STD	Median	STD	Kernel	Median	STD
Original	10.9	30.4	−0.3	32.5	Original	1.2	47.9
Linear	**−3.2**	**26.9**	**−0.3**	**29.0**	Linear	−3.4	38.2
RBF	11.0	27.6	−7.5	33.5	WM+GM (linear)	**−0.8**	**37.3**

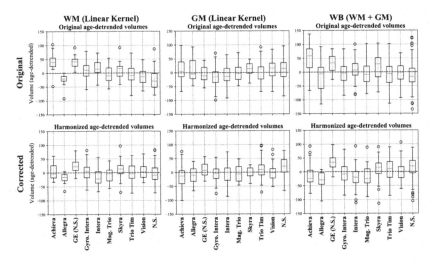

Fig. 3. Distribution of the validation set volumes (mL) before (top) and after (bottom) RVM-based correction using a linear kernel. (N.S.: Not Specified)

Fig. 2). Analysing these correlations reveals that image descriptors like NMI and CNR are related to scanner/acquisition specific features. These same image descriptors are in turn correlated to the brain volumes, as well as scale.

4.2   Harmonization of Healthy Population Data Based on RVM

We trained and tested the RVM method described in Sect. 3 for linear regression on the data set of healthy subjects (Sect. 2). We used different kernel types (linear and Gaussian - RBF) and searched for the model that best preserved biological information - namely age - while decreasing the scanner/center-specific variability. Thus, the model should decrease global variance in the data but maintain the original median of the population defined by the training set, given that we build on the assumption that this sample contains enough variability to represent the heterogeneity of scanner and center effects. To evaluate the performance, we produced boxplots to represent the distribution of the measured

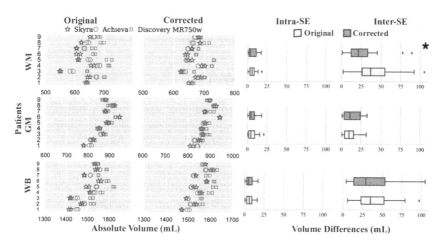

Fig. 4. Difference between same patient brain volumes (mL) acquired in different scanner types. Left: Absolute volumes for each patient before and after correction. Right: Distribution of differences between the Intra-SE and Inter-SE volumes from same patient before and after correction

volumes in each scanner in the test set with at least ten subjects (see Fig. 3). We first removed the age dependency as estimated from the training set, such that the variability due to age is not accounted for. We compare median and standard deviation, preferring values closer to zero, since they represent a decrease in variability while preserving the global trend. Table 1 presents the median values of these same age-detrended values. After correction the distributions from different scanners become more similar. For both GM and WM the linear kernel produced lower or comparable mean and decreased standard deviation. For WB we compared applying a linear kernel to summing the previously corrected WM and GM volumes and verified that the last option performed better.

4.3 Harmonization of Test-Retest Data

To further validate the method, we applied it to the test-retest dataset of MS patients described in Sect. 2. The results are summarized in Fig. 4. On the left side, the absolute volumes before and after correction are represented. First we computed for each tissue type the differences between the volumes from images acquired in the same scanner, which provides a measure of the intra-scanner error (Intra-SE). There is no significant difference between the original and corrected volumes for all the tissue types ($p > 0.05$, paired t-test). Then we computed the difference between the averaged volumes of each scanner type against all the other scanner types. For WM there is a statistically significant difference ($p = 2e^{-3}$, paired t-test) between the original and corrected volumes. For GM, the inter-scanner error (Inter-SE) for the original volumes was very small, being comparable to the Intra-SE. After applying the correction, there is no statistical difference between these volumes and the original ones, even if visually there is an increase in the variability which is propagated for the WB.

5   Conclusions and Future Work

In this work we applied a relevance vector machine approach to find the amount of variability in the data that can be explained by variations in image descriptors. We observe that there is a large dependency of brain volumes with the atlas-registered NMI metric, which was initially not expected. NMI measures the goodness of a non-rigid registration step between the image and an atlas, necessary for the methodology we used. The final volumes depend on the goodness of this registration, and in such a way we are correcting for suboptimal segmentation results that derive from a poor registration step.

We demonstrate that it is possible to achieve a certain degree of harmonization of the data based only on image descriptors. To our knowledge, this is the first approach that does not rely on scanner-specific information to perform harmonization. We expect the current method to perform less efficiently than more tailored methods, but to generalize better. A thorough comparison to such methods still needs to be performed, but it is out of the scope of the current paper. This type of solution is interesting for large scale statistics, and could potentially have a positive impact in longitudinal studies. Moreover, the proposed approach allows dealing with missing scanner/center information, a problem not addressed in previous works and very frequent in practice. Nevertheless, in the test-retest setting inter-scanner error is still high when compared to the measured intra-scanner error, which implies that the method does not provide a completely satisfactory correction for patient specific use, and should be further investigated.

Future steps include exploring more image descriptive features that are independent from the segmentation method used and that can encode the presence of geometrical distortions and artifacts. For controlled environments it could be useful to couple general scanner-dependent information with the image descriptors. Additionally, we aim to extend the method to other brain structures of interest and to compare its performance on a controlled dataset to scanner-specific state-of-the art methods. Finally, it is important to keep in mind that in a cross-sectional setting this type of correction does not replace the need for an improved standardization at the image level.

References

1. Bermel, R.A., Bakshi, R.: The measurement and clinical relevance of brain atrophy in multiple sclerosis. Lancet Neurol. **5**(2), 158–170 (2006)
2. Biberacher, V., et al.: Intra- and interscanner variability of magnetic resonance imaging based volumetry in multiple sclerosis. NeuroImage **142**, 188–197 (2016). https://doi.org/10.1016/j.neuroimage.2016.07.035
3. Biomedical Image Analysis Group, Imperial College London: Ixi dataset. https://brain-development.org/ixi-dataset/. Accessed on 18 Mar 2019

4. Chen, J., et al.: Exploration of scanning effects in multi-site structural MRI studies. J. Neurosci. Methods **230**, 37–50 (2014). https://doi.org/10.1016/j.jneumeth.2014.04.023

5. Chua, A.S., et al.: Handling changes in MRI acquisition parameters in modeling whole brain lesion volume and atrophy data in multiple sclerosis subjects: comparison of linear mixed-effect models. NeuroImage: Clin. **8**, 606–610 (2015)

6. Fortin, J.P., et al.: Harmonization of cortical thickness measurements across scanners and sites. NeuroImage **167**, 104–120 (2018). https://doi.org/10.1016/j.neuroimage.2017.11.024

7. Jain, S., et al.: Automatic segmentation and volumetry of multiple sclerosis brain lesions from MR images. NeuroImage: Clin. **8**, 367–375 (2015). https://doi.org/10.1016/j.nicl.2015.05.003

8. Jones, B.C., et al.: Quantification of multiple-sclerosis-related brain atrophy in two heterogeneous MRI datasets using mixed-effects modeling. NeuroImage: Clin. **3**, 171–179 (2013). https://doi.org/10.1016/j.nicl.2013.08.001

9. MacKay, D.J.C.: Bayesian interpolation. Neural Comput. **4**(3), 415–447 (1992). https://doi.org/10.1162/neco.1992.4.3.415

10. Marcus, D.S., et al.: Open access series of imaging studies (oasis): cross-sectional mri data in young, middle aged, nondemented, and demented older adults. J. Cogn. Neurosci. **19**(9), 1498–1507 (2007)

11. Nyúl, L.G., Udupa, J.K.: On standardizing the MR image intensity scale. Magn. Reson. Med. **42**(6), 1072–1081 (1999)

12. Robitaille, N., Mouiha, A., Crépeault, B., Valdivia, F., Duchesne, S.: Tissue-based MRI intensity standardization: application to multicentric datasets. Int. J. Biomed. Imaging **2012**, 1–11 (2012)

13. Salat, D., et al.: Age-associated alterations in cortical gray and white matter signal intensity and gray to white matter contrast. NeuroImage **48**(1), 21–28 (2009)

14. Takao, H., Hayashi, N., Ohtomo, K.: Effect of scanner in longitudinal studies of brain volume changes. J. Magn. Reson. Imaging **34**(2), 438–444 (2011). https://doi.org/10.1002/jmri.22636

15. Tipping, M.E.: Sparse Bayesian learning and the relevance vector machine. J. Mach. Learn. Res. **1**(3), 211–244 (2001). https://doi.org/10.1162/15324430152748236

16. Zhuge, Y., Udupa, J.K.: Intensity standardization simplifies brain MR image segmentation. Comput. Vis. Image Understand. **113**(10), 1095–1103 (2009). https://doi.org/10.1016/J.CVIU.2009.06.003

Data Pooling and Sampling of Heterogeneous Image Data for White Matter Hyperintensity Segmentation

Annika Hänsch[1]([✉]), Bastian Cheng[2], Benedikt Frey[2], Carola Mayer[2], Marvin Petersen[2], Iris Lettow[2], Farhad Yazdan Shenas[2], Götz Thomalla[2], Jan Klein[1], and Horst K. Hahn[1]

[1] Fraunhofer MEVIS, Bremen, Germany
`annika.haensch@mevis.fraunhofer.de`
[2] Universitätsklinikum Hamburg-Eppendorf, Hamburg, Germany

Abstract. White Matter Hyperintensities (WMH) are imaging biomarkers which indicate cerebral microangiopathy, a risk factor for stroke and vascular dementia. When training Deep Neural Networks (DNN) to segment WMH, data pooling may be used to increase the training dataset size. However, it is not yet fully understood how pooling of heterogeneous data influences the segmentation performance. In this contribution, we investigate the impact of sampling ratios between different datasets with varying data quality and lesion volumes. We observe systematic changes in DNN performance and segmented lesion volume depending on the sampling ratio. If properly chosen, a single DNN can accurately segment and quantify both large and small lesions on different quality test data without loss of performance compared with a specialized DNN.

Keywords: White matter hyperintensity · Segmentation · Data pooling

1 Introduction

Cerebral microangiopathy is a risk factor for several common diseases. It is related to 20% of strokes and is the most common cause for vascular dementia [8]. Adequate treatment can reduce the risk, therefore early detection and systematic quantification are important for prevention. White Matter Hyperintensities (WMH) are an imaging biomarker closely linked to microangiopathy [3]. As the manual segmentation of brain lesions is both time-consuming and subject to high inter-observer variability, automatic segmentation methods are

Electronic supplementary material The online version of this chapter (https://doi.org/10.1007/978-3-030-32695-1_10) contains supplementary material, which is available to authorized users.

© Springer Nature Switzerland AG 2019
L. Zhou et al. (Eds.): OR 2.0 2019/MLCN 2019, LNCS 11796, pp. 86–94, 2019.
https://doi.org/10.1007/978-3-030-32695-1_10

highly desirable [2]. Automated reader-independent and ideally data quality-independent quantification of WMH could also contribute to a more standardized assessment of microangiopathy, improving cross-study comparability and accelerating the clinical applicability of research [11].

The use of Deep Neural Networks (DNN) has become a powerful tool for automatic segmentation also in the neuro domain [1,4]. Yet, as MRI is used for WMH imaging, the training data contrast and quality can vary significantly depending on MR scanner and sequence. Furthermore, depending on the study population, the mean lesion volume can vary significantly. While pooling of data is a common technique especially in the case of small individual datasets, the impact of data heterogeneity on the data-driven DNN training is not yet fully understood.

Data pooling from multiple imaging systems and studies is a challenge, not only for WMH segmentation. Notably, Li et al. [5] have investigated the pooling of data from three MR scanners for WMH segmentation. They found that pooling can improve the segmentation performance compared with training on a single dataset. In their work, each of the datasets contained only 20 cases which may have contributed to the improvement by pooling in addition to the increased training data heterogeneity.

Concerning test data heterogeneity, Moeskops et al. [7] showed that a DNN can accurately and reliably segment WMH and brain tissues in the presence of artifacts and anatomical abnormalities. The algorithm was evaluated on two different cohorts: elderly patients with low expected WMH volume and patients from a memory clinic with comparably larger WMH volume.

In this contribution, we propose to also explore the impact of sampling heterogeneous data during the DNN training on different cohorts. Specifically, we investigate the pooling of heterogeneous data with large WMH lesions from multiple sites and data of healthy subjects with small WMH lesions from an epidemiological study with homogeneous imaging settings. To the best of our knowledge, we are the first to systematically vary the sampling of pooled data from different studies during training for WMH segmentation. We aim to determine whether a single DNN can be used to segment and quantify lesions from different datasets without loss of performance compared with a DNN specialized for each dataset.

2   Methods

2.1   Datasets

Fluid-attenuated inversion recovery (FLAIR) MRI data from three studies was used to build two training and test sets (see supplementary material for an assessment of the data heterogeneity). For all image volumes, reference segmentations of WMH were created by 3 neurological readers trained in the evaluation of MR imaging data of patients with cerebrovascular diseases. In summary, WMH were first detected by a semi-automated procedure based on signal intensities in FLAIR and subsequently refined by visual inspection and manual correction.

All lesion masks were checked by two raters independently and consent achieved consulting a third investigator in cases of severe disagreement.

The Hamburg City Health Study (HCHS)[1] is a large ongoing epidemiological study aiming to investigate risk factors of 26 common diseases including stroke and dementia. Reference WMH segmentations were available for 88 subjects, all scanned on a 3T Siemens scanner with a 3D FLAIR sequence. The axial resolution was 0.75×0.9 mm^2 and slice thickness was 0.75 mm. The median WMH reference volume was 0.55 ml (IQR 1.87 ml).

The CONNECT study was a single center, cross-sectional study of patients with significant cerebral small vessel disease to investigate the association between cerebral macro- and microperfusion and cognitive impairment. Patients with age over 50 and moderate or severe degree of WMH detected by FLAIR MRI were included. Reference WMH segmentations were available for 18 subjects, all scanned on a 3T Siemens scanner with a 2D FLAIR sequence. The axial resolution was 0.72×0.72 mm^2 and slice thickness was 5 mm. The median WMH reference volume was 27.97 ml (IQR 31.15 ml).

WAKE-UP [10] was a multi-center trial including subjects with an unknown time of onset of stroke. Reference WMH segmentations were available for 68 subjects, scanned on different scanner types from Siemens (36 subjects), Philips (30 subjects) and GE (2 subjects) using different 2D FLAIR sequences. Field strengths were 3T (51 subjects) or 1.5T (17 subjects). The axial resolution ranged from 0.43×0.43 mm^2 to 0.94×0.94 mm^2 and slice thickness from 3 mm to 5 mm. The median WMH reference volume was 16.21 ml (IQR 13.65 ml).

2.2   Training and Test Set Composition

A homogeneous training dataset denoted D_{ho} was created using 64 cases of the HCHS study. The remaining 24 HCHS cases were part of the homogeneous test set T_{ho}. The only two subjects with lesion volumes larger than 15 ml were assigned to T_{ho}. The remainder was assigned randomly within two discrete lesion volume classes (0–5 ml, 5–15 ml).

A heterogeneous training dataset denoted D_{he} and a test set T_{he} were created mainly from WAKE-UP and CONNECT. The training set D_{he} contained 55 cases from both studies and T_{he} contained the remaining 31 cases. To increase the variability of T_{he} with respect to small lesions, 9 random cases of T_{ho} were added to T_{he} to reach a total of 40 heterogeneous test cases. The split into T_{he} and D_{he} was not completely random but was based on scanner types, hyper-intense image artifacts and discrete lesion volume classes to achieve a high heterogeneity of the test set. As a general rule, outliers in the data (e.g. acquired on a scanner with less than 4 available subjects) were assigned to the test set in order to increase its heterogeneity and ability to measure robustness of the trained DNNs to unseen data.

---

[1] http://hchs.hamburg/.

2.3   Data Pre-processing

To homogenize the data from different scanners, gray values were normalized by mapping the 5th and 95th gray value percentiles to 0 and 1. Quantiles were computed only within the brain because of varying contrast to surrounding tissue for different MR sequences. Due to large differences in slice thickness, images were resampled only in the transverse plane to 1 mm^2 but not between slices, so that distortions of the fine lesion reference contours were reduced. Consequently, a 2D network architecture was used (see Sect. 2.4).

2.4   Deep Neural Network

As the focus of this work is the impact of training data and sampling rather than architecture optimization, we chose the well-known U-Net architecture [9] with 4 resolution levels for all experiments. The 2D variant was chosen over 3D based on the properties of the training, see Sect. 2.3. All U-Nets were trained to convergence using the Dice loss [6]. The best performing state of the trained weights was chosen based on the Jaccard coefficient computed during each validation step.

2.5   Sampling Scheme

The sampling scheme described in this section is the basis for all results presented in Sect. 3. Let X denote the random variable which describes a sampled training patch and $D_L \subset D_{ho} \cup D_{he}$ the set of all training patches containing true positive lesion voxels. Training patches were sampled so that

$$P(X \in D_{ho}) = p_{ho} \text{ and } P(X \in D_L) = 0.5, \tag{1}$$

where $p_{ho} \in [0,1]$ is the probability of sampling patches from the homogeneous dataset D_{ho}. The probability of sampling a patch with at least one lesion voxel was 50%. Our aim is to evaluate the impact of p_{ho} on the trade-off between DNN specificity versus generalizability to various data qualities and lesion volumes.

3   Results

3.1   Segmentation Performance

A boxplot of the Dice scores between reference and segmentation result per sampling ratio p_{ho} is shown in Fig. 1. On the heterogeneous test set T_{he}, the median Dice scores are within 0.68 ± 0.02 for all $p_{ho} \leq 0.9$. The median Dice scores decrease when less patches are sampled from D_{he}. For $p_{ho} \leq 0.8$, the inter-quartile range (IQR) varies less than 0.05 Dice, with a steep increase for larger p_{ho}. This suggests that the DNN remains robust on T_{he}, even if only 20% of the training patches reflect the high heterogeneity and lesion volume. For larger p_{ho}, the segmentation becomes unreliable (lower mean Dice and larger

IQR). On the homogeneous test set T_{ho}, the median Dice scores increase up to $p_{ho} = 0.6$. For any higher sampling rates from D_{ho}, the median Dice scores are within 0.66 ± 0.02 with the maximum at $p_{ho} = 0.9$. The lowest IQR is reached for $p_{ho} \in [0.6, 0.8]$, where it varies by only 0.01 Dice. This suggests that a DNN can segment small lesions on a homogeneous test set even if up to 40% of the training set are of different data and lesion quality. The most stable performance (lowest IQR), is reached for $p_{ho} \in [0.6, 0.8]$. In summary, our results suggest that using a sampling rate of $p_{ho} \in [0.6, 0.8]$ (lower/upper bound derived from T_{ho}/T_{he}), a DNN can robustly segment large and small lesions on homogeneous and heterogeneous test data without loss of (Dice) performance compared with a specialized network ($p_{ho} \in \{0, 1\}$) and with good stability of the performance (low IQR of Dice scores). Qualitative segmentation results are shown in Fig. 2.

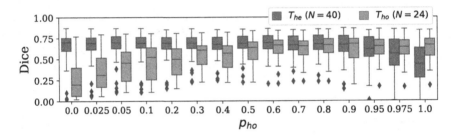

Fig. 1. Dice scores depending on the probability p_{ho} of sampling patches from the homogeneous dataset D_{ho}. Note that the lesions in the homogeneous test set T_{ho} are small (see Sect. 3.2), therefore a single misclassified voxel on average leads to a higher decrease of the Dice score than on the heterogeneous test set T_{he}.

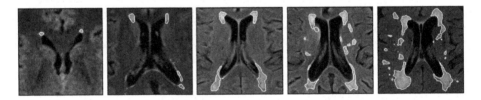

Fig. 2. Reference annotation (yellow overlay) and DNN segmentation (white contour) for $p_{ho} = 0.7$ for test cases of varying lesion volume. (Color figure online)

The Dice score does not reveal whether too many or too few voxels are labeled as lesions. Therefore, we plot the median voxel-wise precision and recall per p_{ho} in Fig. 3. On T_{he}, the increase in precision (P) is approximately linear with the decrease in recall (R), with the two extremes $(P, R, p_{ho}) = (0.64, 0.78, 0)$ and $(P, R, p_{ho}) = (0.90, 0.33, 1)$. However, the change in recall and precision is non-linear with the sampling rate p_{ho}: sampling only 2.5% of patches from D_{he}

accounts for roughly half of the difference in recall and precision between the two extremes $((P, R, p_{ho}) = (0.76, 0.55, 0.975))$.

On T_{ho}, median precision and recall follow a non-linear relationship. For $p_{ho} \leq 0.1$, precision increases and recall decreases with increasing p_{ho} with their minimum and maximum respectively at $(P, R, p_{ho}) = (0.11, 0.89, 0)$. This suggests a strong overestimation of lesions when no data from D_{ho} is sampled during training. For increasing $p_{ho} \geq 0.1$, precision and recall both tend to increase, although there is no clear optimum for $p_{ho} \geq 0.5$. The expectation of improving on T_{ho} by sampling more data from D_{ho} is only true as long as $p_{ho} \leq 0.5$. This means that up to 50% of training patches can be sampled from independent data with different quality and lesion volume statistics without lowering precision and recall. On both test sets, median precision and recall are clustered together for the previously identified range of $p_{ho} \in [0.6, 0.8]$. This supports the observation based on the Dice score, that the exact sampling ratio within this range is not crucial to the overall performance of the DNN.

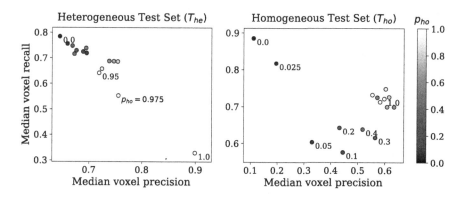

Fig. 3. Median voxel precision versus recall depending on the sampling rate p_{ho}. On T_{he}, precision and recall are linearly correlated. On T_{ho}, precision and recall values are clustered for all $p_{ho} \geq 0.5$. By adjusting p_{ho}, one can adjust the DNN performance.

3.2   Lesion Volume Measurement

The total lesion volume is a quantitative measurement which can directly be computed from the predicted lesion mask. To compare the predicted against the reference lesion volume per test case, we compute the relative volume error $E_r = (\sum_i r_i - \sum_i p_i)/\sum_i r_i$, where r_i and p_i denote the voxels of the binary reference and predicted lesion masks. Figure 4 plots the quartiles of all volume errors per test set against the sampling rate p_{ho}. Note, that the median reference lesion volumes are 14.20 ml on T_{he} and 0.56 ml on T_{ho}. Hence, a large relative error on T_{ho} still is a small absolute error.

On T_{he}, the median predicted volume deviates less than 10% from the reference volume for $p_{ho} \in [0.4, 0.95]$ and by more than 12% for values of p_{ho} close or equal to 0 or 1. For values $p_{ho} \in [0.6, 0.8]$, the median error amounts to 1–4%. On T_{ho}, all median errors are negative which means that the predicted volume tends to be too high. An explanation might be that typical small hyper-intense false positives have a higher impact due to the low total lesion volume. It also cannot be ruled out that especially tiny lesions are missed during the annotation.

We also compute Spearman's rank-order correlation coefficient ρ between reference and predicted lesion volume. A value of 1 indicates a monotonic relationship between the measurements. This is relevant, as monotony means that an increase in volume can be measured using a DNN even if the predicted volume differs from the true volume. The resulting correlations with confidence intervals are shown in Fig. 4. On T_{he}, the correlation and confidence are similar ($\rho = 0.95 \pm 0.01$) for all $p_{ho} \in [0.05, 0.9]$. On T_{ho}, the correlation increases up to $\rho = 0.98$ for $p_{ho} \geq 0.8$. This shows that the lesion volume measurements are accurate and highly correlated with the reference when using suitable sampling rates. Including the results on T_{he}, this shows that a single DNN trained with $p_{ho} \in [0.8, 0.9]$ (lower/upper bound derived from T_{ho}/T_{he}) can quantify large and small WMH on heterogeneous data.

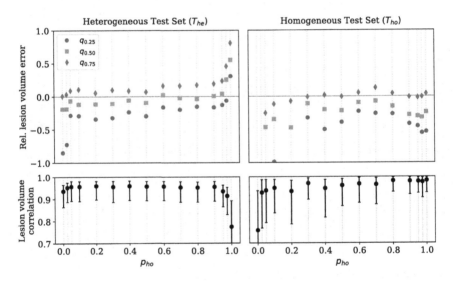

Fig. 4. Top row: Quartiles of the relative lesion volume error on both test sets. Four data points on T_{ho} are cut off for better visualization. Bottom row: Spearman's correlation coefficient between reference and predicted lesion volumes. Error bars indicate a 95% confidence interval of the correlation computed via bootstrapping. Low relative errors and high correlation indicate an accurate lesion volume measurement for suitable values of p_{ho}.

4 Discussion

Overall, our results suggest that a single DNN can segment large and small WMH without loss of performance compared with a specialized DNN ($p_{ho} \in \{0, 1\}$). However, the sampling ratio needs to be chosen appropriately. While on our data, sampling 60–80% of homogeneous patches seemed optimal with respect to Dice scores, these numbers may differ significantly for other datasets. Still, we could observe systematic changes in performance with the sampling rate, which indicates that non-random sampling of pooled data may be superior to random sampling, which is often done in practice. Our results confirm the expectation that a training set which is more similar to the test set will generally lead to better results, but we did not expect the performance (especially on the heterogeneous test set) to be as robust against a large variation of the training set introduced by the sampling. Moreover, we could quantify lesion volumes with high accuracy. Because of the high Spearman correlation indicating monotony, the trained DNNs might also be suitable for processing of follow-up data.

The reported Dice scores do not yet reach the best results (on other test data) of the WMH Segmentation challenge [4]. This may be because we put the focus on data and sampling and did not yet fully optimize the architecture nor made use of ensembles nor used T1 data. The reason for using a fixed architecture and training procedure was to preserve comparability across experiments. For future work, verification of our results with a more advanced architecture would be interesting. However, we would still expect a similar influence of the sampling ratio on the predicted lesion volumes.

A limitation of our work is that two factors may impact the results: the data heterogeneity with respect to quality and acquisition parameters on the one hand and with respect to lesion volumes on the other hand. It is unclear how much of the changes in performance can be attributed to one or the other. Changes in segmented lesion volume depending on the sampling rate indicate an influence of the training sets' lesion volumes. Moreover, despite best efforts to build heterogeneous training and test sets, sample sizes were still too small to investigate the impact of data parameters such as field strength or scanner type in detail. In this work, we chose to include any outliers into the test set to increase its heterogeneity. An alternative would be to use a random split and to perform cross-validation to test on all available cases.

Finally, in this work we looked at sampling rates between pooled datasets when training a new DNN. For future work, it would be interesting to combine this with other techniques such as Transfer Learning to improve existing DNNs.

Acknowledgements. The authors received funding from the German Federal Ministry for Economic Affairs and Energy (Grant No. ZF4173705CR7 and No. ZF4434802CR7) and from the European Union Seventh Framework Program (Grant No. 278276). We gratefully acknowledge the support of NVIDIA Corporation with the donation of the Titan Xp GPU used for this research.

References

1. Akkus, Z., et al.: Deep learning for brain MRI segmentation: state of the art and future directions. J. Digit. Imaging **30**(4), 449–459 (2017). https://doi.org/10.1007/s10278-017-9983-4
2. Ashton, E.A., et al.: Accuracy and reproducibility of manual and semiautomated quantification of MS lesions by MRI. J. Magn. Reson. Imaging **17**(3), 300–308 (2003). https://doi.org/10.1002/jmri.10258
3. Debette, S., Markus, H.S.: The clinical importance of white matter hyperintensities on brain magnetic resonance imaging: systematic review and meta-analysis. BMJ **341**, c3666 (2010). https://doi.org/10.1136/bmj.c3666
4. Kuijf, H.J., et al.: Standardized assessment of automatic segmentation of white matter hyperintensities; results of the WMH segmentation challenge. IEEE Trans. Med. Imaging (2019). https://doi.org/10.1109/TMI.2019.2905770
5. Li, H., et al.: Fully convolutional network ensembles for white matter hyperintensities segmentation in MR images. NeuroImage **183**, 650–665 (2018). https://doi.org/10.1016/j.neuroimage.2018.07.005
6. Milletari, F., et al.: V-Net: fully convolutional neural networks for volumetric medical image segmentation. In: 4th International Conference on 3D Vision (3DV), pp. 565–571. IEEE (2016). https://doi.org/10.1109/3DV.2016.79
7. Moeskops, P., et al.: Evaluation of a deep learning approach for the segmentation of brain tissues and white matter hyperintensities of presumed vascular origin in MRI. NeuroImage: Clin. **17**, 251–262 (2018). https://doi.org/10.1016/j.nicl.2017.10.007
8. Pantoni, L.: Cerebral small vessel disease: from pathogenesis and clinical characteristics to therapeutic challenges. Lancet Neurol. **9**(7), 689–701 (2010). https://doi.org/10.1016/S1474-4422(10)70104-6
9. Ronneberger, O., Fischer, P., Brox, T.: U-Net: convolutional networks for biomedical image segmentation. In: Navab, N., Hornegger, J., Wells, W.M., Frangi, A.F. (eds.) MICCAI 2015. LNCS, vol. 9351, pp. 234–241. Springer, Cham (2015). https://doi.org/10.1007/978-3-319-24574-4_28
10. Thomalla, G., et al.: MRI-guided thrombolysis for stroke with unknown time of onset. N. Engl. J. Med. **379**(7), 611–622 (2018). https://doi.org/10.1056/NEJMoa1804355
11. Wardlaw, J.M., et al.: Neuroimaging standards for research into small vessel disease and its contribution to ageing and neurodegeneration. Lancet Neurol. **12**(8), 822–838 (2013). https://doi.org/10.1016/S1474-4422(13)70124-8

A Hybrid 3DCNN and 3DC-LSTM Based Model for 4D Spatio-Temporal fMRI Data: An ABIDE Autism Classification Study

Ahmed El-Gazzar[1(✉)], Mirjam Quaak[1,2], Leonardo Cerliani[1], Peter Bloem[2], Guido van Wingen[1], and Rajat Mani Thomas[1]

[1] Department of Psychiatry, Amsterdam UMC, University of Amsterdam, Amsterdam, The Netherlands
a.g.elgazzar@amsterdamumc.nl
[2] Vrije Universiteit Amsterdam, Amsterdam, The Netherlands

Abstract. Functional Magnetic Resonance Imaging (fMRI) captures the temporal dynamics of neural activity as a function of spatial location in the brain. Thus, fMRI scans are represented as 4-Dimensional (3-space + 1-time) tensors. And it is widely believed that the spatio-temporal patterns in fMRI manifests as behaviour and clinical symptoms. Because of the high dimensionality ($\sim$1 Million) of fMRI, and the added constraints of limited cardinality of data sets, extracting such patterns are challenging. A standard approach to overcome these hurdles is to reduce the dimensionality of the data by either summarizing activation over time or space at the expense of possible loss of useful information. Here, we introduce an end-to-end algorithm capable of extracting spatiotemporal features from the full 4-D data using 3-D CNNs and 3-D Convolutional LSTMs. We evaluate our proposed model on the publicly available ABIDE dataset to demonstrate the capability of our model to classify Autism Spectrum Disorder (ASD) from resting-state fMRI data. Our results show that the proposed model achieves state of the art results on single sites with F1-scores of 0.78 and 0.7 on NYU and UM sites, respectively.

Keywords: Deep learning · ASD · 3D convolutions · 3D convolutional-LSTM · rs-fMRI

1 Introduction

Unlike other fields of medicine, psychiatry lacks diagnostic criteria based on validated biomarkers. Finding these biomarkers is critical for (i) understanding the underlying neural causes, (ii) improving diagnosis and (iii) predicting treatment outcome. Functional magnetic resonance imaging (fMRI)—a well-established proxy for neural activity—is often taunted as a promising non-invasive technique

© Springer Nature Switzerland AG 2019
L. Zhou et al. (Eds.): OR 2.0 2019/MLCN 2019, LNCS 11796, pp. 95–102, 2019.
https://doi.org/10.1007/978-3-030-32695-1_11

that has enough information in them to design a robust biomarker. This information, often present as spatio-temporal patterns in fMRI is challenging to extract given its dimensionality (~1 Million) and typical data volumes (typically <200 samples/subjects at any given center). In this paper we focus on Autism Spectrum Disorder (ASD). ASD represents a heterogeneous group of developmental brain disorders characterized by lifelong social deficits and repetitive behaviour.

Deep learning, because of its recent success in a multitude of tasks, is being currently explored in neuroimaging. For example in classifying Alzheimer, and predicting disease conversion [11]. The key advantage of deep learning is its ability to learn useful features from raw data; eliminating the need for subjective feature design as required by "classical" machine learning techniques. But applying deep learning to fMRI has been problematic because of the issue of dimensionality and data volume.

To overcome these issues fMRI data are often reduced in dimension either by summarizing brain activity spatially or temporally. In the classification of ASD versus controls for example, several studies convert the full 4-D resting-state fMRI (rs-fMRI) signal in to a correlation matrix. These matrices are based on the average time course within regions-of-interest (ROI) given by an atlas [1,8,9]. Instead of averaging over time, Dvornek et al. [6] used long short-term memory (LSTM) cells on the timeseries of 200 selected brain regions for the same task. Similarly, [7] applied 1D convolutions on extracted timeseries of different atlases. Alternatively, Li et al. [10] directly learned spatial features from the 3D fMRI images, but reduced the temporal information by taking the mean and standard deviation of fixed time windows. These subjective feature selection methods could drastically reduce the ability to detect complex patterns in neural activity and may lead to suboptimal results.

Instead, we propose to learn end-to-end from the full 4D fMRI sequences using a framework that takes advantage of both spatial and temporal information in the data to achieve the objective. On the ABIDE dataset, we show that our approach can surpass subjective methods that rely on feature engineering and we also avoid any procedure to summarize data.

2   Method

In this work we present a novel architecture for 4D rs-fMRI data with application to ASD classification. We utilize the strength of convolutional LSTMs (C-LSTM) in spatio-temporal feature extraction by employing a 3D variant in our proposed pipeline. Further, we demonstrate another variation of architecture that does not use convolutional LSTMs. Since LSTMs are computationally expensive, we propose a computationally cheaper alternative with a 1D convolution for spatio-temporal processing. The idea of this variant was inspired by [7] that demonstrated the capability of 1D convolutions to extract useful features from time courses of rs-fMRI for the diagnosis of ASD. In addition, the comparison of these two models helps to identify the contribution of the convolutional LSTMs.

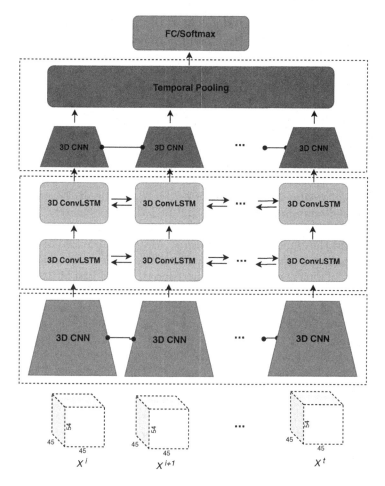

Fig. 1. Overview of the proposed deep architecture. 3DCNN and bidirectional C-LSTM are used to learn the spatial and long-term spatiotemporal features, following which a 3DCNN is used to learn higher-level spatiotemporal features based on the learnt 3D long-term spatiotemporal feature maps for the final classification layer.

2.1 3DCNN_C-LSTM

The main challenge in employing recurrent neural networks (RNN) in fMRI is the high dimensionality of the data. The spatial dimension of a 4 mm down-sampled volume in MNI space is $45 \times 54 \times 45$, where the size of the time-series depends on the duration of the scan and the TR, and usually ranges from 100 to 400 time points. Together with the limited sample sizes, classical RNNs fail to train efficiently on the raw 4D volumes. One alternative is to reduce the spatial dimensions first, but that is likely to remove informative local/temporal features. To overcome this issue, we design an end-to-end pipeline that enables efficient training of RNNs in high dimensional environments. Our pipeline consists of three components:

3D CNN for Spatial Feature Learning: The 3D CNN component in the proposed architecture is a shallow CNN with 4 convolutional layers. The purpose of this component is: (1) to reduce the spatial dimension of the original volume for efficient training of the recurrent layers. (2) extract lower level spatial feature maps necessary for spatio-temporal feature learning at the next stage. We use a 3D CNN with tied weights at all the input time steps for coherent spatial feature extraction and efficient training.

The kernel size of each CNN layer is $3 \times 3 \times 3$ with stride $2 \times 2 \times 2$ to downsample the input feature vector. We add dropout with a rate of 0.2 to the output of every convolution to regularize the network.

3D C-LSTM for Spatio-Temporal Feature Learning: One of the most common choices to model temporal sequences is the LSTM. Unfortunately, LSTMs take a sequence of vectors as inputs. This would require us to flatten our spatial dimensions, and thus ignore spatial patterns. Moreover, the LSTM applies fully connected transformations to these vectors, leading to very large weight matrices, unless the spatial dimensions are strongly reduced. The C-LSTM [12] solves both problems: it replaces the fully connected vector-transformations by convolutions, allowing us to model the temporal information in a memory efficient way, without flattening the spatial dimensions.

The inputs $X_1, \ldots, X_t$, the cell states $C_1, \ldots, C_t$, the hidden states $H_1, \ldots, H_t$ and the gates i_t, f_t, o_t of C-LSTM are all 4D tensors. Let $*$ denote the convolution operator, and let $\otimes$ denote the Hadamard product. The C-LSTM can be formulated as:

$$i_t = \sigma(W_{xi} * X_t + W_{hi} * H_{t-1} + b_i)$$
$$f_t = \sigma(W_{xf} * X_t + W_{hf} * H_{t-1} + b_f)$$
$$o_t = \sigma(W_{xo} * X_t + W_{ho} * H_{t-1} + b_o)$$
$$C_t = f_t \otimes C_{t-1} + i_t \tanh(W_{xc} * X_t + W_{hc} * H_{t-1} + b_c)$$
$$H_t = o_t \otimes \tanh(C_t)$$

Where σ is the sigmoid function, and all weight matrices W are 3D convolution kernels. The convolutions in the C-LSTM have kernel size 3×3 with stride 1×1. "Same-Padding" is used to ensure that the spatiotemporal feature maps in each C-LSTM layer have the same spatial size. A two-layer bidirectional C-LSTM is constructed as illustrated in Fig. 1 to encode global temporal information and local spatial information into 3D spatio-temporal feature maps.

3D CNN for Higher Level Spatio-Temporal Feature Learning: Since the 3D spatiotemporal feature maps still have large spatial size, dimensionality reduction is necessary for the final classification. Another simple 3DCNN with tied weights is employed to reduce the dimensionality further and to learn the higher-level spatiotemporal features, based on the learnt 3D spatiotemporal feature maps at each recurrent step of C-LSTM. Only a shallow 3DCNN is constructed in this implementation. Nevertheless, deeper 3DCNNs can also be used for different configurations or applications.

2.2   3DCNN_1D

1D convolutions offer a simpler alternative to LSTMs with longer effective memory [2]. They have been successfully applied to capture the temporal dynamics of the fMRI signal for ASD classification [7]. Therefore, this alternative model applies a 1D convolution for spatio-temporal feature learning after the 3D CNN component. The first layers for spatial feature learning are similar to the 3DCNN_C-LSTM model. After the 3D convolutional layers, a global average pooling layer is added to yield a 1D vector with the length of the input time-series. One 1D Convolution is applied on this vector with the learned spatial features as input channels. Hereafter, a temporal pooling layer as in the C-LSTM model is conducted to summarize the temporal information followed by a fully connected layer to output the classification probabilities.

3   Experiments and Results

3.1   Datasets

We use the publicly available ABIDE dataset to evaluate our proposed pipeline. We preprocessed the data with the Configurable Pipeline for the Analysis of Connectomes (C-PAC) and the fMRI volumes are downsampled to 4 mm in MNI. We use single sites to evaluate the network capacity to learn the spatio-temporal features with a small sample size but uniform scanning parameters. We also experiment with the multi-site data provided from ABIDE-I dataset to test the network performance in a heterogeneous environment but a larger sample size. For single sites experiments, we use the NYU and UM sites from ABIDE-I. Those provide the highest number of balanced (ASD/typically developing (TD)) subjects with 184 and 110 subjects respectively. For the multi-site experiment we used ABIDE-I with 19 sites and 1100 subjects.

3.2   Network Training

The proposed architectures are trained in an end-to-end fashion from scratch. To speed up training and to increase the diversity of samples seen by the model, we select a random contiguous sub-sequence of 20 time points for each instance (re-sampling every epoch). For validation and testing, the full time-series per subject are used by feeding subsequent crops to the model and average the predictions over all crops. We train our models for 500 epochs with a batch size of 8. For optimization of the cross entropy loss function, we employ the Adam optimizer with a learning rate of 0.0001. During training, we evaluate the performance on the validation set every 10 epochs and use the best model for evaluation.

3.3   Results and Comparison with State-of-the-Art

We compare our models to previous deep learning ABIDE classification models that handled the temporal and spatial dimensions in different ways and achieved the best results reported thus far. We report the results for the models in Table 1 on the respective dataset. We reran the best reported experiments from [8] and using the recommended settings and available code on our dataset and report the results. For [7] we used the full time-series for single-site experiments and selected for and cropped to 100 timepoints for the ABIDE-I dataset. For [3] we report the results for the models on the NYU site from their paper. We provide a short description of the models and input data type.

- **AE_MLP** [8]: uses correlation matrices of the extracted time-courses from the Craddock atlas [4] to pre-train a stacked fully-connected autoencoder and fine tune it for classification.
- **SVM** [5]: uses the same input features as **AE_MLP** to train a support vector machine with an rbf kernel.
- **1DConv** [7]: uses extracted time courses from the Harvard Oxford atlas as input to a 1D convolutional neural network.
- **CNN3D_TC** [3]: 3D spatial data is used in a 3D convolutional network where the temporal information is stacked as channels.
- **CNN3D_MD** [3]: same approach as CNN_TC but only mean and standard deviation of the temporal dimension are stacked as channels.
- **convGRU_CNN3D** [3]: uses the 4D volume where spatio-temporal information are processed by a 3D convolutional GRU followed by a 3D CNN.
- **CNN4D** [3]: uses 4D convolutions on the 4D volumetric data.

We report 5-fold cross validation mean F1-score and accuracy for the experiments in Table 1. The results show that the proposed architecture 3DCNN_C-LSTM outperforms other models on single site experiments by achieving mean test accuracies and F1 scores of 0.77 and 0.78 respectively for the NYU site and 0.71 and 0.7 on the UM site. This surpasses previous methods by 10% and 8% for NYU and UM sites respectively.

3DCNN_C-LSTM however also shows a degraded performance in multi-site environment as evidenced by the results on ABIDE-1 data that features 19 sites. We attribute the loss of performance of our model to the heterogeneity of the data acquired from different scanners with different scanning parameters. This effect does not show in other methods that do not use the full 4D volumes where data preprocessing and summarization play an important role in input signal consistency and hence model generalization.

Our results for the 3DCNN_1D shows inferior performance compared to using C-LSTMs in all three datasets. This supports the vital role of a recurrent module in the network for spatio-temporal feature processing. However, the competitive performance of this architecture with the 1DConv model shows the ability of our first 3DCNN to extract useful spatial features in an end-to-end fashion compared to using pre-computed atlases.

Table 1. 5-fold cross validation mean accuracies and F1-scores of trained models on NYU, UM and ABIDE-I data

Data	Model	Accuracy	F1-score
NYU	AE_MLP [8]	0.64 ± 0.1	0.67
	SVM [5]	0.6 ± 0.13	0.59
	1D_Conv [7]	0.64 ± 0.11	0.62
	CNN3D_TC* [3]	0.57	0.61
	CNN3D_MS* [3]	0.60	0.65
	convGRU-CNN3D* [3]	0.67	0.71
	CNN4D* [3]	0.60	0.68
	3DCNN_1D (ours)	0.59 ± 0.07	0.58
	3DCNN_C-LSTM (ours)	**0.77 ± 0.05**	**0.78**
UM	AE_MLP [8]	0.56 ± 0.11	0.59
	SVM [5]	0.54 ± 0.11	0.56
	1D_Conv [7]	0.63 ± 0.1	0.62
	3DCNN_1D (ours)	0.66 ± 0.09	0.58
	3DCNN_C-LSTM (ours)	**0.71 ± 0.06**	**0.70**
ABIDE-I	AE_MLP [8]	0.63 ± 0.02	0.64
	SVM [5]	0.58 ± 0.04	0.6
	1D_Conv [7]	**0.64 ± 0.06**	**0.64**
	3DCNN_1D (ours)	0.54 ± 0.02	0.50
	3DCNN_C-LSTM (ours)	0.58 ± 0.03	0.53

*Results as reported by Bengs et al. [3] on NYU data.

4   Discussion

We have introduced a deep architecture that extracts information from fMRI signals for the classification of ASD, using 3DCNN and bidirectional 3DC-LSTMs; allowing the network to exploit local and global spatio-temporal structures. The proposed deep architecture provides an alternative method to hard-coded features or summary measures to reduce the dimensionality. The paper only presents the preliminary version of the deep architecture. The 3DCNN and C-LSTM networks can be further improved in order to obtain higher classification accuracy. This architecture can also be used as a starting point for domain adaption techniques that can be deployed to boost the performance on multi-site data by compensating for data heterogeneity when using the full 4D volumes.

Acknowledgement. This work was supported by the Netherlands Organization for Scientific Research (NWO; 628.011.023), Philips Research, AAA Data Science Program, and ZonMW (Vidi; 016.156.318).

References

1. Abraham, A., et al.: Deriving reproducible biomarkers from multi-site resting-state data: an autism-based example. NeuroImage **147**, 736–745 (2017)
2. Bai, S., Kolter, J.Z., Koltun, V.: An empirical evaluation of generic convolutional and recurrent networks for sequence modeling. arXiv preprint arXiv:1803.01271 (2018)
3. Bengs, M., Gessert, N., Schlaefer, A.: 4D spatio-temporal deep learning with 4D fMRI data for autism spectrum disorder classification (2019). Extended Abstract MIDL https://openreview.net/forum?id=HklAUVnV5V
4. Craddock, R.C., James, G.A., Holtzheimer III, P.E., Hu, X.P., Mayberg, H.S.: A whole brain fMRI atlas generated via spatially constrained spectral clustering. Hum. Brain Mapp. **33**(8), 1914–1928 (2012)
5. Cristianini, N., Shawe-Taylor, J., et al.: An Introduction to Support Vector Machines and Other Kernel-Based Learning Methods. Cambridge University Press, Cambridge (2000)
6. Dvornek, N.C., Ventola, P., Pelphrey, K.A., Duncan, J.S.: Identifying autism from resting-state fMRI using long short-term memory networks. In: Wang, Q., Shi, Y., Suk, H.-I., Suzuki, K. (eds.) MLMI 2017. LNCS, vol. 10541, pp. 362–370. Springer, Cham (2017). https://doi.org/10.1007/978-3-319-67389-9_42
7. El Gazzar, A., Cerliani, L., van Wingen, G., Mani Thomas, R.: Simple 1-D convolutional networks for resting-state fMRI based classification in autism, July 2019
8. Heinsfeld, A.S., Franco, A.R., Craddock, R.C., Buchweitz, A., Meneguzzi, F.: Identification of autism spectrum disorder using deep learning and the ABIDE dataset. NeuroImage: Clin. **17**, 16–23 (2018)
9. Khosla, M., Jamison, K., Kuceyeski, A., Sabuncu, M.: 3D convolutional neural networks for classification of functional connectomes. arXiv preprint arXiv:1806.04209 (2018)
10. Li, X., et al.: 2-channel convolutional 3D deep neural network (2CC3D) for fMRI analysis: ASD classification and feature learning. In: 2018 IEEE 15th International Symposium on Biomedical Imaging (ISBI 2018), pp. 1252–1255. IEEE (2018)
11. Vieira, S., Pinaya, W.H., Mechelli, A.: Using deep learning to investigate the neuroimaging correlates of psychiatric and neurological disorders: methods and applications. Neurosci. Biobehav. Rev. **74**, 58–75 (2017)
12. Shi, X., Chen, Z., Wang, H., Yeung, D.Y., Wong, W.K., Woo, W.C.: Convolutional LSTM network: a machine learning approach for precipitation nowcasting. In: Advances in Neural Information Processing Systems, pp. 802–810 (2015)

Automated Quantification of Enlarged Perivascular Spaces in Clinical Brain MRI Across Sites

Florian Dubost[1(✉)], Max Dünnwald[2,3], Denver Huff[2], Vincent Scheumann[2], Frank Schreiber[2], Meike Vernooij[1,5], Wiro Niessen[1,6], Martin Skalej[4], Stefanie Schreiber[2], Steffen Oeltze-Jafra[2,7], and Marleen de Bruijne[1,8(✉)]

[1] Department of Radiology and Nuclear Medicine, Erasmus MC, Rotterdam, The Netherlands
floriandubost1@gmail.com, marleen.debruijne@erasmusmc.nl
[2] Department of Neurology, Otto-von-Guericke University Magdeburg, Magdeburg, Germany
[3] Faculty of Computer Science, Otto-von-Guericke University Magdeburg, Magdeburg, Germany
[4] Department of Neuroradiology, Otto-von-Guericke University Magdeburg, Magdeburg, Germany
[5] Department of Epidemiology, Erasmus MC, Rotterdam, The Netherlands
[6] Department of Imaging Physics, Faculty of Applied Science, TU Delft, Delft, The Netherlands
[7] Center for Behavioral Brain Sciences (CBBS), Magdeburg, Germany
[8] Department of Computer Science, University of Copenhagen, Copenhagen, Denmark

Abstract. Enlarged perivascular spaces (PVS) are structural brain changes visible in MRI, and are a marker of cerebral small vessel disease. Most studies use time-consuming and subjective visual scoring to assess these structures. Recently, automated methods to quantify enlarged perivascular spaces have been proposed. Most of these methods have been evaluated only in high resolution scans acquired in controlled research settings. We evaluate and compare two recently published automated methods for the quantification of enlarged perivascular spaces in 76 clinical scans acquired from 9 different scanners. Both methods are neural networks trained on high resolution research scans and are applied without fine-tuning the networks' parameters. By adapting the preprocessing of clinical scans, regions of interest similar to those computed from research scans can be processed. The first method estimates only the number of PVS, while the second method estimates simultaneously also a high resolution attention map that can be used to detect and segment PVS. The Pearson correlations between visual and automated scores of enlarged perivascular spaces were higher with the second method. With this method, in the centrum semiovale, the correlation was similar to theinter-rater agreement, and also similar to the performance in high res-

---

F. Dubost and M. Dünnwald—Equal contribution.
S. Oeltze-Jafra and M. de Bruijne—Equal contribution.

© Springer Nature Switzerland AG 2019
L. Zhou et al. (Eds.): OR 2.0 2019/MLCN 2019, LNCS 11796, pp. 103–111, 2019.
https://doi.org/10.1007/978-3-030-32695-1_12

olution research scans. Results were slightly lower than the inter-rater agreement for the hippocampi, and noticeably lower in the basal ganglia. By computing attention maps, we show that the neural networks focus on the enlarged perivascular spaces. Assessing the burden of said structures in the centrum semiovale with the automated scores reached a satisfying performance, could be implemented in the clinic and, e.g., help predict the bleeding risk related to cerebral amyloid angiopathy.

Keywords: Perivascular spaces · Deep learning · Clinical MRI

1   Introduction

Enlarged perivascular spaces (PVS) are structural brain changes visible on MRI. They can be identified as thin hyperintense tubular structures on T2-weighted MRI scans. PVS are increasingly thought to reflect the presence of cerebral small vessel disease, which represents a leading cause of cognitive decline and functional loss in elderly patients. In most studies, enlarged perivascular spaces are quantified using visual scores that either classify the burden of PVS in several categories [8], or count PVS [1]. These quantification methods are tedious and observer-dependent. Recently, several methods have been proposed to automatically quantify PVS burden [2,4–6,10,13]. None of these methods have been evaluated in clinical scans, which present multiple challenges for the quantification of PVS. While in research studies, the scanning is highly standardized (same machine, same protocol, same scanning parameters, same investigators, etc.) to yield comparable results, this is not the case in clinical routine. The lower resolution of clinical scans also results in the computation of less accurate shape features, the most discriminative feature for the detection of PVS. Moreover, other MRI markers related to cerebral small vessel disease – such as white matter hyperintensities – are more prevalent in clinical scans than in population studies [2,4–6] and could be confused with PVS because of their similar appearance.

In most studies, PVS are quantified separately in one or several clinically and epidemiologically relevant brain regions: midbrain, hippocampi, thalamus, basal ganglia, and centrum semiovale. In PVS research, the centrum semiovale is the most studied region, as PVS burden there has been most strongly associated to potential determinants of PVS and outcomes thereof. The centrum semiovale is also often the region with highest inter-observer agreement in the visual scoring of PVS [1]. In this study, we quantified PVS in the hippocampi, basal ganglia, and centrum semiovale.

Zhang et al. [13] automatically quantified PVS on 7T MRI scans. Boespflug et al. [2] proposed an automated quantification method combining image intensities and morphologic features from several MRI sequences. They evaluated their method in the centrum semiovale in research scans. Sudre et al. [10] proposed to use recurrent neural networks to detect PVS and lacunar infarcts in 16 subjects of a longitudinal study investigating the relationship between cardiovascular risk factors and brain health. van Wijnen et al. [11] regressed intensity distance maps of PVS in the centrum semiovale using neural networks. Recently, Dubost et al. [4] proposed to quantify PVS burden in four brain regions – midbrain, hippocampi, basal ganglia, and centrum semiovale – with neural network regressors trained with image level labels: the count of PVS in the target brain region. In research scans, the authors showed that they could reach a correlation between visual scores and automated scores similar to that of the inter-observer agreement in each region. They also found that associations between 20 determinants of PVS and visual PVS scores, and between the same determinants and automated PVS scores, were similar. The same authors [5] proposed to use a more advanced model (GP-Unet) for weakly supervised detection of enlarged perivascular spaces. This method estimates simultaneously the number of PVS and a high resolution attention map that can be used to detect and segment PVS. We decided to study the methods of Dubost et al. [4,5] as the validation experiments with associations with clinical variables already brought them one step ahead of other methods for the application to clinical practice.

In this article, we applied and compared the two methods of Dubost et al. [4,5] on 76 clinical MRI scans with a varying, low resolution acquired in the clinical routine of a hospital using nine different scanners and different protocols, while using models' weights learned from high-resolution population study MRI scans acquired at another hospital in a highly controlled and standardized setting using a single scanner and protocol. The networks were not fine-tuned to the clinical data. For preprocessing, we used FSL packages instead of FreeSurfer parcellations of [4,5] to segment the regions of interest. Finally, we show examples of attention maps of GP-Unet.

2 Datasets

Training Data. The training data consists of 1600 T2-weighted MRI scans from 1600 elderly participants in a population study: the Rotterdam Study [7]. Scans were acquired on a single 1.5T GE scanner, in a highly controlled and standardized setting. The scan resolution was $0.5 \times 0.5 \times 0.8 \, \text{mm}^3$. PVS were visually scored by a single rater in all scans in the hippocampi, basal ganglia and centrum semiovale, following the guidelines of Adams et al. [1].

Table 1. Characteristics of the clinical dataset (minimum, maximum, mean and standard deviation)

	Min	Max	Mean	Std
Patient age (years)	35	89	71.39	9.32
In-plane (axial) resolution (mm^2)	0.39	0.68	0.45	0.04
Resolution in z (mm)	3.30	7	4.94	0.89
Spacing between slices (mm)	0.60	6.60	4.73	1.04

Evaluation Data. The MRI data used for evaluation were gathered retrospectively from the Picture Archiving and Communication System (PACS) of University Hospital Magdeburg. MRI scans with visible signs of cerebral small vessel disease were selected. All selected patients had cerebral microangiopathy, and were diagnosed with at least one of the following: ischemic (i.e. lacunar) stroke or transient ischemic attack, spontaneous intracerebral hemorrhage, dementia (i.e. Alzheimer's disease or vascular dementia), and epileptic seizures. Initially, 100 acquisitions from 100 different patients were collected. 24 Scans were excluded from the experiments either because FSL segmentation of the brain structures failed or because scans could not be rated visually, e.g. due to insufficient image quality caused by motion artifacts or presence of other pathologies such as extremely large lesions. This leaves a total of 76 scans for the study. Since the acquisitions have been obtained during the clinical routine, they present a considerable variance with respect to various image properties such as artifacts or image resolution. T1-weighted and T2-weighted MRI scans have been acquired with 9 different scanners. Two of these scanners, a 3T and a 1.5T from Philips, make up 66 of the 76 images. In total, there are three 3T-, four 1.5T- and two 1T-scanners. Three of them were Siemens (two 3T, one 1.5T), the rest were Philips machines. The time frame in which the data was acquired is almost 15 years and ranges from August 2004 until March 2019. The majority of the scans (43) has been acquired within the last 5 years of this period. The number of male and female patients was 46 and 30, respectively. Table 1 provides additional information about the data set. PVS were scored visually in the hippocampi, basal ganglia and centrum semiovale following the guidelines of Adams et al. [1]. Two raters scored PVS, the inter-rater agreement is reported in Table 2.

3   Methods

The target brain regions (hippocampi, basal ganglia, and centrum semiovale) are first segmented, masked and cropped. The result is then processed by trained convolutional neural networks that predict the count of PVS in each region. The neural networks were trained with high resolution MRI scans of a population study, but were used to predict PVS count in routine clinical scans of a hospital. The study was approved by the local ethics committee (No 28/16).

3.1   Preprocessing

To match the resolution of scans in the training set, all clinical scans were linearly interpolated to a resolution of $0.5 \times 0.5 \times 0.8\,mm^3$.

Dubost et al. [4] used FreeSurfer parcellations to segment brain regions. FreeSurfer brain parcellation lasts usually several hours, which may prevent its use in clinical routine. In this study, we used instead FIRST and FAST algorithms from the FSL package [9] to segment brain regions from the T1 sequence in a matter of minutes. FIRST could compute segmentation of the basal ganglia and hippocampi. FAST was used to segment the white matter for the centrum

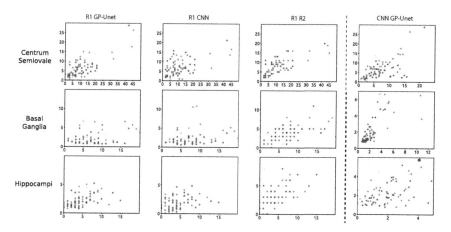

Fig. 1. Comparison between visual and automated PVS scores. The different colors represent different scanners. The visual PVS scores of the first rater (R1), on the x-axis, are compared with the predictions of GP-Unet, CNN, and with the visual scores of the second rater (R2), on the y-axis. In the right column we plotted the automated PVS scores of GP-Unet versus those of CNN.

semiovale region. Dubost et al. [4] also evaluated their method in the midbrain. As midbrain segmentation is not implemented in FSL, this region was excluded from the study. The T1 sequence was then rigidly registered to the T2 sequence using FSL FLIRT, and the segmentation labels were propagated from the T1 space to the T2 space.

Following the guidelines of Adams et al. [1] for visual scoring of PVS, Dubost et al. [4] quantified PVS in the centrum semiovale in the neighborhood of the slice located 1 cm above the top of the lateral ventricles. As FSL does not compute ventricle segmentation, we used instead the segmentation of the basal ganglia as approximation, and selected the slice 1 cm above the top of the caudate nucleus.

The following preprocessing steps were computed exactly as described by Dubost et al. [4]. Namely, the segmentation masks were dilated, convolved with a gaussian kernel to smooth the border of the mask, and multiplied pixelwise with the T2 intensities. The masked regions were then cropped, normalized between 0 and 1 using the minimum and maximum intensity values in the masked region, and given as input to the neural networks.

3.2   Neural Networks

The preprocessed images were given as input to two different types of neural networks proposed for automated PVS quantification: (1) a neural network with four convolutional layers and a max-pooling layer which outputs the number of PVS in a region [4] and that we call *CNN*, and (2) *GP-Unet*, a similar neural network proposed by the same authors [5], in which the downsampling path is followed by an upsampling path to enable weakly supervised detection of PVS. Networks of both methods were trained with only image-level labels.

Attention maps of GP-Unet were computed to visualize the focus of the networks using a linear combination of the feature maps of the last convolutional layer, as described by Dubost et al. [5].

4   Results and Discussion

Table 2 shows the Pearson correlation, and Table 3 the mean absolute error, between visual and automated PVS scores for each region and for each method, and the corresponding inter-rater agreement. Scatter-plots are shown in Fig. 1. Attention maps of GP-Unet are displayed for each region in Fig. 2.

There was no noticeable difference in the computation of the regions of interest when using FSL masks instead FreeSurfer masks, but the interpolation to $0.5 \times 0.5 \times 0.8 \, mm^3$ was needed to reuse the networks optimized on high resolution scans. The visual PVS scores were highly correlated to the automated PVS scores of GP-Unet in the centrum semiovale (0.78 Pearson correlation), were moderately correlated in the hippocampi (0.52), and a lower correlation in the basal ganglia (0.28). Attention maps of GP-Unet (Fig. 2) show that, as expected, the method focuses on perivascular spaces.

While on research scans, CNN and GP-Unet reached a similar performance in all regions, our experiments on clinical scans show that the correlation between visual PVS scores and automated PVS scores of GP-Unet was significantly higher than that of visual PVS scores and automated scores of CNN in the centrum semiovale (Williams' test, p-value < 0.0001) and in the hippocampi (p-value < 0.05). Contrary to CNN, GP-Unet combines features of different scales via skip connections, which may have assisted the computation of discriminative shape features, and improved the detection of single PVS, as opposed to detecting – or missing because of their too large size – a cluster of PVS without being able to individually count them.

The correlation in the basal ganglia (0.31 for GP-Unet) is lower than in the other regions and is notably lower than the inter-rater agreement (0.56). Attention maps (Fig. 2) show that the network only detects the largest PVS in the basal ganglia, and misses less enlarged PVS. The scatter-plots (Fig. 1) seem

Table 2. Correlation between visual and automated PVS scores. Pearson correlations between the first rater and GP-Unet, CNN, and the second rater for each region. Correlations were all significant (p-value < 0.01). Significant correlations after Bonferroni correction are in bold.

	GP-Unet	CNN	R2
Centrum Semiovale	**0.78**	**0.52**	**0.75**
Basal Ganglia	0.31	0.25	**0.56**
Hippocampi	**0.51**	0.33	**0.64**

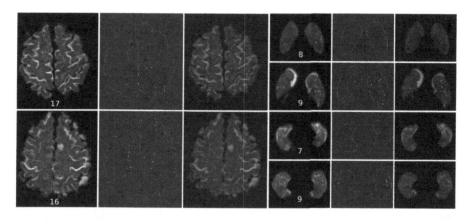

Fig. 2. Attention Maps of GP-Unet in an axial view. Attention maps for the centrum semiovale are displayed on the left, for the basal ganglia on the top right, and for hippocampi, on the bottom right. Visual scores are indicated below each region. For each selected image, from left to right, we show the original image, the attention map with drawn contours of the region, and the overlay of both. The colormaps of the attention maps were manually adjusted for each image. Highlighted structures are considered as PVS by the networks. The redder a structure is, the higher is its weight in the computation of the automated PVS scores by the network. For the centrum semiovale, we selected two images that correspond to an average agreement between automated and visual score (human rater R1). For the basal ganglia and hippocampi, we selected one image with poor agreement (top), and another image with good agreement (bottom).

to confirm this observation: in the basal ganglia, the networks underestimate the number of PVS, and predict similarly low numbers of PVS for all scans.

Table 2 shows lower inter-rater agreement for the basal ganglia than for the other regions. This might be a consequence of PVS being visually rated only in a single slice in this region [1]. The low resolution of clinical scans in z direction might cause a large variability in the selection of this slice, which might negatively influence the reproducibility of the visual rating. The automated methods quantify PVS in the complete volume of the basal ganglia, which was previously shown to be more reproducible than the visual PVS scores [6]. Interestingly, the automated PVS scores of both methods – CNN and GP-Unet – are highly correlated in the basal ganglia (0.73 Pearson correlation). The correlation between their scores was higher in the basal ganglia than in other regions.

Results in the centrum semiovale (0.78 Pearson correlation) are similar to the inter-rater agreement (0.75). This is also close to the inter-rater agreement (0.80 intraclass correlation coefficient) as reported in earlier studies in high resolution research scans [1]. Demonstrated quantification of PVS burden in the centrum semiovale could aid in the better stratification of cerebral small vessel disease subtypes, i.e. hypertensive arteriopathy and cerebral amyloid angiopathy, especially in large and hospital-based cohorts. This would presumably have important therapeutic and prognostic implications in terms of prescribing oral

Table 3. Mean absolute errors between visual and automated PVS scores. Mean absolute error between the first rater and GP-Unet, CNN, and the second rater for each region.

	GP-Unet	CNN	R2
Centrum Semiovale	5.58	6.39	4.67
Basal Ganglia	5.67	5.49	3.78
Hippocampi	2.58	3.0	2.08

anticoagulants and preventing intracerebral hemorrhage. This is of particular importance in cerebral amyloid angiopathy, that has not only been related to severe PVS burden in the centrum semiovale [3], but also to a significantly higher risk for intracerebral bleeding in face of oral anticoagulant treatment [12].

In future work, the results in the basal ganglia and the hippocampi may be improved by fine-tuning the neural networks using the clinical dataset, and by adding data augmentation during training with research scans to imitate the resolution of clinical scans and contrast variations between different scan protocols or scanners. The results presented are already promising considering the large differences between training and test sets.

The complete computation of the automated PVS scores lasts only a few minutes on CPU. Most of the computation time is spent on FSL brain structures segmentation and registration from the T1-weighted scans to the T2-weighted scans. After this preprocessing, the computation of the automated PVS scores took only about 6 s per brain region on CPU. This low computation time can facilitate the implementation of such a method in clinical practice.

5   Conclusion

We showed that PVS burden could be automatically quantified in the centrum semiovale in clinical scans, with an agreement with visual scores that was similar to the inter-observer agreement. Automated PVS scores were computed with a neural network that was trained high-quality research scans and with only global labels of PVS burden. These results could contribute to bringing automated PVS quantification to the clinic and guide the administration of anti-coagulant drugs.

Acknowledgements. This work received funding from the Netherlands Organisation for Health Research and Development (ZonMw - Project 104003005) and the federal state of Saxony-Anhalt, Germany (Project I 88).

References

1. Adams, H.H., et al.: Rating method for dilated Virchow-Robin spaces on magnetic resonance imaging. Stroke **44**(6), 1732–1735 (2013)

2. Boespflug, E.L., et al.: MR imaging-based multimodal autoidentification of perivascular spaces (mMAPS): automated morphologic segmentation of enlarged perivascular spaces at clinical field strength. Radiology **286**(2), 632–642 (2017)
3. Charidimou, A., et al.: MRI-visible perivascular spaces in cerebral amyloid angiopathy and hypertensive arteriopathy. Neurology **88**(12), 1157–1164 (2017)
4. Dubost, F., et al.: Enlarged perivascular spaces in brain MRI: automated quantification in four regions. NeuroImage **185**, 534–544 (2019)
5. Dubost, F., et al.: Weakly Supervised Object Detection with 2D and 3D Regression Neural Networks. arXiv preprint arXiv:1906.01891 (2019)
6. Dubost, F., et al.: 3D regression neural network for the quantification of enlarged perivascular spaces in brain MRI. Med. Image Anal. **51**, 89–100 (2019)
7. Ikram, M.A., et al.: The Rotterdam Study: 2018 update on objectives, design and main results. Eur. J. Epidemiol. **32**(9), 807–850 (2017)
8. Potter, G.M., et al.: Cerebral perivascular spaces visible on magnetic resonance imaging: development of a qualitative rating scale and its observer reliability. Cerebrovasc. Dis. **39**(3–4), 224–231 (2015)
9. Smith, S.M., et al.: Advances in functional and structural MR image analysis and implementation as FSL. Neuroimage **23**, S208–S219 (2004)
10. Sudre, C.H., et al.: 3D multirater RCNN for multimodal multiclass detection and characterisation of extremely small objects. In: MIDL 2019 (2018)
11. van Wijnen, K.M., et al.: Automated lesion detection by regressing intensity-based distance with a neural network. In: MICCAI (2019)
12. Wilson, D., et al.: Cerebral microbleeds and intracranial haemorrhage risk in patients anticoagulated for atrial fibrillation after acute ischaemic stroke or transient ischaemic attack (CROMIS-2): a multicentre observational cohort study. Lancet Neurol. **17**(6), 539–547 (2018)
13. Zhang, J., Gao, Y., Park, S.H., Zong, X., Lin, W., Shen, D.: Segmentation of perivascular spaces using vascular features and structured random forest from 7T MR image. In: Wang, L., Adeli, E., Wang, Q., Shi, Y., Suk, H.-I. (eds.) MLMI 2016. LNCS, vol. 10019, pp. 61–68. Springer, Cham (2016). https://doi.org/10.1007/978-3-319-47157-0_8

Correction to: Live Monitoring of Haemodynamic Changes with Multispectral Image Analysis

Leonardo A. Ayala, Sebastian J. Wirkert, Janek Gröhl,
Mildred A. Herrera, Adrian Hernandez-Aguilera, Anant Vemuri,
Edgar Santos, and Lena Maier-Hein

Correction to:
Chapter 5 in: L. Zhou et al. (Eds.): *OR 2.0 Context-*
Aware Operating Theaters and Machine Learning in
Clinical Neuroimaging, **LNCS 11796,**
https://doi.org/10.1007/978-3-030-32695-1_5

The chapter "Live Monitoring of Haemodynamic Changes with Multispectral Image Analysis", written by Leonardo A. Ayala, Sebastian J. Wirkert, Janek Gröhl, Mildred A. Herrera, Adrian Hernandez-Aguilera, Anant Vemuri, Edgar Santos, and Lena Maier-Hein, was originally published without open access.

Following the author's/authors' decision to opt for open access, the copyright of the chapter changed on 14 November 2023 to © Authors, 2023 and the chapter is now distributed under the terms of the Creative Commons Attribution.

The updated version of this chapter can be found at
https://doi.org/10.1007/978-3-030-32695-1_5

© The Author(s) 2024
L. Zhou et al. (Eds.): OR 2.0/MLCN 2019, LNCS 11796, pp. C1–C2, 2024.
https://doi.org/10.1007/978-3-030-32695-1_13

Open Access This chapter is licensed under the terms of the Creative Commons Attribution 4.0 International License (http://creativecommons.org/licenses/by/4.0/), which permits use, sharing, adaptation, distribution and reproduction in any medium or format, as long as you give appropriate credit to the original author(s) and the source, provide a link to the Creative Commons license and indicate if changes were made.

The images or other third party material in this chapter are included in the chapter's Creative Commons license, unless indicated otherwise in a credit line to the material. If material is not included in the chapter's Creative Commons license and your intended use is not permitted by statutory regulation or exceeds the permitted use, you will need to obtain permission directly from the copyright holder.

Author Index